CLIFFTON SANTIAGO

Cultural Chameleons

The Adaptive Mind

To the generous souls who welcomed me with warmth and kindness, sharing their homes, cultures, and stories, thank you for the invaluable education and unforgettable wonders you bestowed upon me. Your openness and hospitality have enriched my journey in ways words cannot fully capture.

This book is dedicated to all the adventurers and kindred spirits I've met along the way. Your passion for life, learning, and growth has inspired me to embrace each moment and melt into the human experience.

"Not all those who wander are lost."

J.R.R. TOLKIEN

Contents

Preface

In the vast expanse of our world, amidst the myriad hues of cultures and landscapes, there exists a timeless dance of exploration and discovery. It is a dance that I've been privileged to partake in, wandering through bustling streets, traversing tranquil valleys, and immersing myself in the rich warmth of humanity's collective story.

As I reflect on my journey, from the bustling favelas of Brazil to the one of snowiest regions of the world in Hokkaido Japan, I am reminded of the profound beauty that lies in the intersections of diverse cultures. Each encounter, each conversation, has been a brushstroke in the masterpiece of my experiences, painting a portrait of boundless curiosity.

Through the lens of cultural immersion, I've witnessed the transformative power of adaptability, a skill honed not through textbooks or classrooms, but through the visceral experience of navigating unfamiliar terrain, both literal and metaphorical. It is a skill born of necessity, forged from new encounters and unexpected challenges.

And yet, in the heart of the chaos and cacophony of our world, there exists a quiet wisdom, a universal truth that transcends language and borders. It is the understanding that beneath our external differences lies a shared humanity, a common thread that binds us all together in our mutual existence.

In the pages that follow, I invite you to join me on a journey of exploration and introspection, a journey that delves into the heart of what it means to be a cultural chameleon in a world of endless possibility. Together, let us wander through the labyrinthine alleyways, taste the flavors of distant lands, and bask in the warmth of unfamiliar smiles.

For in the act of embracing diversity, we not only enrich our own lives but also contribute to the mosaic of human experience, one that is as vast and varied as the stars in the night sky. So let us set forth on this odyssey of discovery, for the world is waiting, and there is magic to be found in every corner, if only we have the eyes to see and the heart to feel.

Our journey begins with a simple truth: that the world is a palette painted with the colors of countless cultures, each one unique and yet interconnected, each one offering a glimpse into the vastness of human creativity and expression. From the ancient civilizations of the Nile Valley to the modern metropolises of the Far East, from the indigenous tribes of the Amazon rain forest to the nomadic herders of the Mongolian steppe, our world is a treasure trove of diversity waiting to be discovered.

But to truly appreciate the richness of such a mention, we must be willing to step outside of our comfort zones, to venture beyond the familiar and embrace the unknown. It is in these moments of exploration, of pushing the boundaries of our own understanding, that we discover the true depth and beauty of the world around us.

For me, this journey began many years ago, with a single step into the unknown as an unaccompanied minor traveling to Europe from North America. And since then I have always been drawn to the idea of travel, of experiencing new cultures and landscapes firsthand, but it wasn't until I was provided such a leap of faith that I truly understood the transformative power of cultural immersion.

And since that moment, the exhilaration of stepping off a plane in a distant land, the sights and sounds of a foreign city enveloping me, the excitement has not abated. I remember the warmth of the smiles that greeted me, the kindness of strangers who welcomed me into their homes and their hearts. And I remember the profound sense of awe and wonder that filled me as I explored the hidden corners of this unfamiliar world, each new discovery igniting a spark of curiosity and joy within me.

But amidst the excitement and adventure, there were also moments of challenge and uncertainty. There were times when I felt lost and alone, when the unfamiliarity of my surroundings left me feeling adrift in a sea of unsettledness. Yet it was in these moments of discomfort that I truly began to understand the importance of adaptability, of being able to navigate the complexities of cultural differences with grace and humility.

Through trial and error, I learned to embrace the unknown, to lean into the discomfort and allow it to shape me into a more resilient and adaptable individual. I learned to listen deeply, to open myself up to new perspectives and ways of thinking, and to find common ground with those whose experiences were vastly different from my own.

And with each new encounter, each new cultural exchange, I discovered something remarkable, that despite our differences, we are all connected by the common threads of our humanity. Whether we hail from the bustling streets of New York City or the remote villages of the Indian Zanskar mountain range, we share at the very core similar hopes and dreams, fears and aspirations that unite us as members of the human family.

In the pages that follow, I invite you to embark on a journey of discovery and self-reflection, a journey that will take you from the bustling night markets of Hong Kong to the national parks of Colombia, from the sun-drenched beaches of Thailand to the grey autumn day canal walks of Amsterdam. Along the way, you will meet an array of colorful characters – from wise elders steeped in ancient traditions to bright-eyed children eager to share their world with you.

You will delve into the manifold expressions of culture found throughout the world, each one a unique expression of the human spirit. You will discover the profound beauty that lies in the intersections of diverse perspectives, and the transformative power of adaptability in navigating the complexities of our modern world.

But more than anything, you will come to understand that the true essence of cultural immersion lies not in the places you visit or the sights you see, but in the connections you forge and the relationships you build along the way. It is in the moments of shared laughter and shared sorrow, of genuine human connection, that you will find the true magic of travel. The magic of becoming a cultural chameleon, able to adapt and thrive in any environment, and to see the world through the eyes of those who call it home.

So let us set forth on this grand adventure together with open hearts and open minds, ready to embrace the wonders that await us. For in the act of exploration, of stepping outside of ourselves and into the unknown, we discover not only the beauty of the world around us, but also the beauty within ourselves. And in that discovery, we find the true essence of what it means to be alive, to be human, to be a part of something greater than ourselves.

1

Echoes of the Global Stage

In the melange of humanity's collective existence, few forces have been as transformative and pervasive as globalization. Over the past century, the world has witnessed an unprecedented surge in interconnectedness, driven by technological advancements, economic integration, and cultural exchange. This phenomenon, often referred to as globalization, has not only reshaped the landscape of international relations and commerce but has also exerted a profound influence on the fabric of societies and cultures worldwide.

At its core, globalization encapsulates the intricate web of interconnectedness that spans across nations, transcending geographical boundaries and cultural barriers. It manifests in myriad forms, from the seamless flow of goods and capital across continents to the instantaneous exchange of information facilitated by digital technologies. In the realm of culture and society, globalization has heralded an era of unprecedented cultural diffusion, wherein ideas, values, and practices traverse the globe with unprecedented ease.

One of the most palpable manifestations of globalization's impact is the phenomenon of cultural homogenization. As societies become increasingly interconnected, cultural boundaries blur, giving rise to a global cultural zeitgeist characterized by a convergence of tastes, trends, and lifestyles. The proliferation of multinational corporations, mass media, and digital platforms has accelerated this process, disseminating Western cultural norms and consumerist ideals to the farthest corners of the earth.

However, alongside the consolidating currents of globalization, there also exists a countervailing force, cultural hybridization. As cultures come into contact with one another, they engage in a dynamic process of cultural exchange, adaptation, and synthesis. This phenomenon is evident in the proliferation of fusion cuisines, multicultural art forms, and hybrid identities that emerge at the intersections of diverse cultural traditions.

In the midst of this cultural flux, fluidity emerges as a quintessential skill for navigating the complexities of a globalized world. In an era marked by rapid change and uncertainty, the ability to evolve and thrive in diverse cultural contexts is not merely advantageous but indispensable. Adaptability encompasses a spectrum of cognitive, emotional, and behavioral traits that enable individuals to effectively navigate unfamiliar environments, negotiate cultural differences, and leverage diversity as a source of enrichment rather than division.

At its essence, a transformational capacity entails a willingness to embrace change, cultivate an open-minded attitude, and cultivate a repertoire of skills and strategies for navigating unfamiliar terrain. It requires a willingness to step outside one's comfort zone, confront ambiguity, and engage in continuous learning and self-reflection. In the context of globalization, resourcefulness transcends mere survival; it represents a pathway to personal growth, professional success, and cross-cultural competence.

Moreover, elasticity is not merely an individual trait but also a collective imperative. In an increasingly interconnected world, the ability of societies and institutions to understand the changing circumstances and embrace diversity is essential for fostering resilience, innovation, and social cohesion. Whether it be in the realms of politics, economics, or social relations, the capacity to accommodate diverse perspectives, values, and interests is paramount for building inclusive and sustainable communities.

In light of these realities, it is evident that foresight is not merely a desirable trait but a necessity for thriving in the globalized world. As cultures converge and collide, individuals and societies alike are called upon to cultivate the tailored mindset and skills necessary to navigate the complexities of our interconnected world. By embracing diversity, fostering cultural fluency, and cultivating a spirit of openness and curiosity, we can harness the transformative potential of globalization to create a more inclusive, equitable, and harmonious world for all.

As we delve deeper into the exploration of adaptability, it becomes evident that its significance transcends individual circumstances, permeating every facet of human existence. Whether in the realm of personal development or professional endeavors, versatility emerges as a linchpin of success, enabling individuals to navigate the complexities of life with resilience, resourcefulness, and grace.

In the context of personal growth, acclimatization serves as a catalyst for self-transformation and empowerment. It empowers individuals to transcend the limitations of their circumstances, embrace change as an opportunity for growth, and chart new pathways towards fulfillment and success. Whether confronting adversity, navigating life transitions, or pursuing ambitious goals, the ability to adapt enables individuals to harness their inner resilience and creativity to surmount challenges and seize opportunities.

Consider the inspiring journey of Lama Dorjay, a young Buddhist monk in Northern India whose unwavering determination and resilience have fueled his extraordinary path of leadership and innovation amidst a maze of challenges and uncertainties. As the first son in his family has was to become a monk, Lama Dorjay then embarked on a profound quest for spiritual growth and cultural exploration.

By the age of 30, he had already assumed the esteemed role of head of a 2000-year-old monastery, a position of profound responsibility and honor. His leadership also transcends the monastery's walls, as he oversees the well-being of a village nestled at a staggering 4000 meters above sea level. In this remote and elevated locale, Lama Dorjay has adeptly embraced modern technology to connect with people across the globe, bridging the gap between his traditional community and the wider world.

Demonstrating a visionary approach, Lama Dorjay has collaborated with Europeans to enhance tourism, recognizing the potential for cultural exchange and economic development. Concurrently, he has partnered with charities to improve the village's infrastructure and education, ensuring a sustainable and prosperous future for his community.

Indeed, Lama Dorjay's journey serves as a poignant reminder of the transformative power of perseverance in the face of adversity. His ability to pivot and adapt amidst uncertainty is a testament to his unwavering spirit. Today, Lama Dorjay stands as a shining example of what can be achieved through resilience, determination, and a willingness to embrace change.

His story resonates far beyond individual achievement, echoing the collective ingenuity of communities and societies throughout history. In times of crisis and upheaval, it is individuals like Lama Dorjay who serve as beacons of hope and inspiration, demonstrating the extraordinary capacity of the human spirit to overcome adversity and forge a path toward a brighter, more prosperous future.

Yet, as Lama Dorjay navigates the complexities of globalization, he finds himself torn between the desire to preserve the sanctity of his ancient culture and the need to evolve towards modern times. The influx of tourism and the introduction of new technologies bring undeniable benefits, but they also pose a threat to the traditional ways of life that have sustained his community for centuries. He grapples with this duality, striving to strike a balance between progress and preservation.

In doing good for the evolution of his culture and environment, Lama Dorjay is acutely aware of the push and pull that comes with living in the realm of globalization. He witnesses firsthand the transformation of his village, where ancient rituals and customs coexist with contemporary practices. This delicate equilibrium requires constant vigilance and a deep understanding of the cultural and spiritual heritage that forms the bedrock of his community.

Ultimately, such a journey is a testament to the intricate dance between change and continuity. He embodies the spirit of adaptability, not by abandoning the old, but by finding ways to integrate the new without losing the essence of what once existed. In his efforts to uplift his community, Lama Dorjay serves as a poignant reminder that the path to progress must be navigated with care, respect, and a profound sense of responsibility towards preserving the unique aspects of different cultures.

Consider the example of Airbnb[1], the pioneering online marketplace for short-term lodging, which revolutionized the hospitality industry through its innovative business model and forward-thinking approach to growth. Founded in 2008

---

[1] Wikipedia contributors. (2024, May 24). *Airbnb*. Wikipedia. https://en.wik ipedia.org/wiki/Airbnb

during the midst of the global financial crisis, Airbnb faced numerous challenges and setbacks in its early years, including regulatory hurdles, funding shortages, and fierce competition from established players.

However, through a combination of strategic pivots, bold experimentation, and relentless perseverance, Airbnb weathered the storm and emerged as a global juggernaut, disrupting the traditional hotel industry and redefining the way people travel and experience new cultures. By embracing change, challenging the status quo, and remaining attuned to the evolving needs and preferences of its customers, Airbnb transformed adversity into opportunity, cementing its status as one of the most iconic success stories of the digital age.

In essence, the power of adaptability lies in its ability to transcend adversity, catalyzing growth, innovation, and resilience in the face of uncertainty and change. Whether at the individual, community, or organizational level, resourcefulness serves as a cornerstone of success, enabling individuals and societies alike to navigate the complexities of life with courage, creativity, and grace. As we embark on our journey towards embracing diversity and cultivating cultural fluency, let us embrace the transformative potential of fluidity as our guiding light, illuminating the path towards a brighter, more inclusive future for all.

In the complexity of human existence, there exists a rich diversity of cultures, languages, and traditions, each contributing to the vibrant array of our global community. Yet, amidst this diversity, a common thread binds us together – our shared humanity, our innate desire for connection, understanding, and belonging. It is in this spirit of unity and empathy that we delve into the transformative power of travel, cultural encounters, and a certain plasticity.

At its core, this exploration aims to articulate a vision of a world where cultural diversity is celebrated, cherished, and embraced as a source of enrichment and strength. Through travel and cultural exploration, we embark on a journey of self-discovery and growth, navigating the complexities of our multicultural world with confidence, curiosity, and empathy.

The aim is not merely to impart knowledge or offer practical tips for navigating cultural differences, but to cultivate an such a mindset that enables us to approach diversity with humility, openness, and a willingness to learn. By embracing adaptability, empathy, and cultural fluency, we enhance our lives and contribute to a more inclusive, harmonious global community.

Central to this ethos is the belief that travel can transform our external world and our internal landscape – shaping our perspectives, expanding our horizons, and deepening our understanding of ourselves and others. Through immersive experiences in diverse cultural environments, we step outside our comfort zones, confront biases, and challenge preconceived notions about the world.

One key objective is to develop a capacity to thrive in the face of uncertainty and change. In today's fast-paced, interconnected world, adaptability emerges as a crucial competency for success.

By cultivating flexibility, resilience, and resourcefulness, we are better equipped to navigate the complexities of our globalized world with confidence.

Moreover, this exploration aims to inspire us to become catalysts for positive change. By embodying dexterity, strength, and cultural fluency, we can bridge divides, foster understanding, and promote social cohesion in an increasingly polarized world.

Through insightful reflections, practical strategies, and real-life examples, we find a road map for embracing diversity, navigating cultural differences, and forging meaningful connections. Whether embarking on solo adventures or engaging in intercultural dialogue at home, we emerge with a renewed sense of purpose and commitment to building a more inclusive world.

In essence, this journey is a call to action, a rallying cry to embrace diversity with an open mind and a compassionate heart. Through the transformative power of travel and adaptability, we have the opportunity to transcend our differences, create meaningful connections, and build a future where all voices are heard and valued. It is my hope that this exploration will inspire and empower readers around the world to embrace diversity and build a more inclusive society for generations to come.

"Tradition is not the worship of ashes, but the preservation of

fire." - Gustav Mahler[2]

---

[2] Quotees. (2024, January 31). *Gustav Mahler – Tradition is not the Worship of Ashes, but the Preservation of Fire – Quote*. Quotees. https://quotees.co.uk/q uotes/gustav-mahler-tradition-is-not-the-worship-of-ashes-but-the-prese rvation-of-fire-quote/

2

Open Doors, Open Minds

In the labyrinth of human interaction, adaptability emerges as a guiding light illuminating the path through the diverse landscapes of globalization. Defined as the capacity to adjust to new conditions, such versatility serves as a cornerstone in navigating the intricate interrelation that characterizes our modern world. It is not merely a passive reaction to external stimuli but rather an active engagement with the ever-changing dynamics of our environment. This empowers individuals to embrace the fluidity of diversity, transcending cultural boundaries and forging connections across disparate realms. In essence, it is the art of seamlessly integrating oneself into the mosaic of humanity's collective existence, weaving threads of understanding and empathy across the fabric of global society.

The importance of which cannot be overstated in the context of navigating diverse environments. In a world where borders blur and cultures converge, the ability to morph becomes a fundamental survival skill. It enables individuals to thrive amidst the complexities of multicultural interactions, transcending linguistic, social, and ideological barriers. Whether traversing the bustling streets of a cosmopolitan metropolis or immersing oneself in the tranquil rhythms of a remote village, refined individuals exhibit a remarkable capacity to acclimate to their surroundings with ease and grace. Their versatility allows them to navigate the nuances of diverse environments, embracing unfamiliar customs and perspectives with an open mind and a generous spirit.

Indeed, such individuals are like chameleons, seamlessly blending into their surroundings while retaining their innate essence. They possess a rare combination of fusion and resilience, allowing them to weather the storms of change and emerge stronger on the other side. In the midst of uncertainty and upheaval, they remain steadfast in their commitment to growth and transformation, turning obstacles into opportunities and challenges into triumphs. Their perseverance as a beacon of hope in a world fraught with discord and division, reminding us of the boundless potential of the human spirit to transcend adversity and forge a brighter tomorrow.

It is essential to recognize the multifaceted dimensions and profound implications of one's constant evolution. Such growth is not a one-size-fits-all concept but rather a complex interplay of psychological, emotional, and cognitive factors. It encompasses a spectrum of traits and skills, ranging from resilience and openness to creativity and innovation. At its core, evolving is about embracing change as a catalyst for growth, embracing diversity as a source of enrichment, and embracing uncertainty as a pathway to discovery. It is about navigating the ebb and flow of life with grace and embracing the myriad possibilities that await us on the horizon.

As we will delve deeper into the essence of such traits, exploring its defining characteristics, its transformative power, and its profound implications for individuals and societies alike. We will examine the psychological and emotional components while uncovering the inner workings of the adaptable mind and the resilient heart. We will also explore the role of travel in cultivating openness, tracing the metamorphic journeys of Cultural chameleons as they navigate the diverse landscapes of our globalized world. Through these explorations, we hope to shed light on the nature of these evolving experiences and inspire readers to embark on their own journey of self-discovery and transformation. For in the ever-evolving story of human existence, warmth and generosity can be the threads that bind us together, weaving a story of resilience, diversity, and possibility.

An malleable nature is not merely a product of external circumstances but is deeply rooted in the psychological and emotional landscape of the individual. At its core, the agile mind is a testament to the resilience of the human spirit, reflecting our capacity to navigate life's complexities with grace and fortitude. As we delve into the psychological and emotional components of one's malleability, we explore the traits and skills that underpin this essential quality.

One of the key psychological traits associated with fluidity is resilience. Resilience can be defined as the ability to bounce back from adversity, to weather the storms of life with courage and perseverance. It is the inner strength that enables individuals to confront challenges head-on, to learn from setbacks, and to emerge stronger and more resilient than before. Resilient individuals possess a sense of optimism and self-efficacy, believing in their ability to overcome obstacles and achieve their goals. They view failure not as a defeat but as an opportunity for growth, seeing each setback as a stepping stone on the path to success.

Another important psychological trait linked to adaptability is openness. Openness refers to a willingness to embrace new experiences, ideas, and perspectives. It is characterized by curiosity, resourcefulness, and a sense of adventure, allowing individuals to explore unfamiliar terrain with an open mind and a receptive heart. Open individuals are not bound by rigid beliefs or preconceived notions but are instead open to the possibility of change and growth. They approach life with a sense of wonder and curiosity, eager to learn from the diverse array of experiences that the world has to offer.

Adroitness is also a crucial psychological component of a nimble mind. It can be defined as the ability to adapt to changing circumstances and to adjust one's thoughts, emotions, and behaviors accordingly. It is the willingness to let go of rigid expectations and to embrace the fluidity of life with an open heart and mind. Chameleonic individuals are able to navigate the twists and turns of life with ease, navigating new situations and challenges with grace and resilience. They are not easily shaken by setbacks or obstacles but instead remain steadfast and resourceful in the face of adversity.

Emotional intelligence plays a vital role in shaping versatility. Emotional intelligence refers to the ability to recognize, understand, and manage our own emotions, as well as the emotions of others. It involves skills such as self-awareness, self-regulation, empathy, and social skills, all of which are essential for navigating the complexities of interpersonal relationships and social dynamics. Emotionally intelligent individuals are adept at recognizing their own emotions and the emotions of others, allowing them to respond appropriately to a wide range of situations and to build strong and meaningful connections with those around them.

At the heart of our potential progression lies a deep sense of self-awareness. Self-awareness is the ability to recognize and understand our own thoughts, feelings, and behaviors, as well as their impact on ourselves and others. It involves introspection and self-reflection, allowing individuals to gain insight into their strengths, weaknesses, and areas for growth. Self-aware individuals are able to recognize when they are feeling overwhelmed or stressed and take steps to manage their emotions and behaviors accordingly. They are also able to recognize their own biases and prejudices and challenge them in order to foster greater understanding and empathy towards others.

In addition to self-awareness, self-regulation is another important component of the adaptive mindset. Self-regulation involves the ability to control our impulses, manage our emotions, and foster stability during changing circumstances with resilience and grace. It requires discipline and self-control, as well as the ability to remain calm and composed in the face of adversity. Self-regulated individuals are able to maintain a sense of equilibrium even in the midst of chaos, allowing them to respond to challenges with clarity and purpose.

Empathy is also a crucial aspect of the adaptable mind. The ability to understand and share the feelings of others, to see the world from their perspective, and to respond with compassion and kindness. It involves not only recognizing the emotions of others but also validating their experiences and offering support and understanding. Empathetic individuals are able to build strong and meaningful relationships with others, fostering trust and cooperation even in the most challenging of circumstances. By way of intent and processing, regardless of a potential opposing opinion.

Finally, social skills play a vital role in shaping flexibility. Social skills refer to the ability to communicate effectively, to build rapport with others, and to navigate social interactions with confidence and ease. They involve skills such as active listening, assertiveness, and conflict resolution, all of which are essential for building strong and resilient relationships with others. Socially skilled individuals are able to collaborate effectively with others, to resolve conflicts constructively, and to build consensus and cooperation even in diverse and multicultural environments.

Returning from Brazil during the 2014 World Cup was an adventure for me and my spouse at the time (both experienced travelers), one that required an extraordinary level of perseverance. Flying standby with no fixed itinerary available meant embracing uncertainty and being ready to pivot at a moment's notice. As we navigated through the chaos of the largest gathering of humanity on the planet, it became clear that our journey home would be anything but straightforward.

After weeks of immersing ourselves in the excitement of the World Cup and organizing every detail of our trip, including accommodations and activities for a group of six, the return journey tested our resolve. Getting bumped from our first flight was just the beginning of our unexpected odyssey. We had to rely on our resourcefulness to find lodging, resorting to questioning the cab stand until we stumbled upon a place to rest for the night, a distant hotel in a not so vibrant part of São Paulo.

As we scrambled to find an alternative route home, we found ourselves booking a flight to Paris, with plans to then travel to Toronto, Canada, effectively crossing the Atlantic twice in one day. Exhausted and disoriented, we arrived at Charles de Gaulle Airport, where fatigue finally caught up with us. I vividly recall trying to consume a croissant prior dozing off on the airport floor, a testament to the sheer exhaustion we were experiencing.

Despite the challenges and setbacks, the unwavering optimism and determination we encompassed shone through. With her persuasive charm and finely developed social skills my travel partner ultimately convinced the crew to upgrade us to first class for the Toronto leg of our journey. The unexpected gesture of comfort, complete with a hug, a glass of cognac, and a plush blanket, was a small but significant reminder of the power of positivity in the face of adversity. Throughout the ordeal, we never once complained, embodying a spirit of grace and composure that helped us navigate the turbulent journey home.

At the crossroads of exploration and transformation lies the profound role of travel in cultivating adaptability. As cultural Cultural Chameleons, we embark on journeys not only to discover new landscapes but also to delve into the depths of our own being, to stretch the boundaries of our comfort zones, and to embrace the richness and diversity of the world around us. Travel serves as a gateway to new experiences and challenges, a crucible in which skills of a certain mental pliability are forged and refined.

One of the most transmutative aspects of travel is its ability to expose individuals to new experiences and challenges. Whether traversing the bustling streets of a vibrant metropolis or trekking through the rugged terrain of a remote wilderness, travel offers a myriad of opportunities to step outside our comfort zones and embrace the unknown. It challenges us to navigate unfamiliar environments, to interact with people from different walks of life, and to confront the complexities of cultural diversity head-on. In the face of these challenges, adaptable individuals rise to the occasion, drawing upon their resourcefulness to navigate the complexities of the road with grace and poise.

Moreover, immersion in different cultures serves as a powerful catalyst for the cultivation of skills with such empowerment. As we engage with people from diverse backgrounds and traditions, we are confronted with a kaleidoscope of perspectives and ways of life, each offering valuable insights into the human experience. Through these interactions, we learn to navigate the nuances of cultural differences with sensitivity and empathy, fostering mutual understanding and respect.

Travel offers a unique opportunity for self-discovery and personal growth. As we step outside our comfort zones and confront the unknown, we are forced to confront our own fears and limitations, to push past the boundaries of what we thought possible, and to embrace the fullness of our potential. We discover that the ease of adjustment is not just about adapting to external circumstances but embracing to the ever-changing landscape of our own inner world, navigating the depths of our own fears and insecurities with courage and compassion.

In the end, the true value of the innate wanderer lies not in the destinations we reach but in the journey itself. It is a journey of self-discovery and personal growth, a journey of connection and transformation, a journey that challenges us to stretch beyond our comfort zones and embrace the richness and diversity of the world around us. As cult Cultural Chameleons, we embrace the unknown with open hearts and open minds, navigating the complexities of the road chosen and emerging stronger, wiser, and more compassionate as a result.

"The art of life lies in a constant readjustment to our surround-ings."
 - Kakuzo Okakura, The Book of Tea[3]

---

[3] Okakura, K. (1912). *The Book of Tea.*

3

Harmony's Canvas - Painting Cultural Understanding

I n delving into the heart of cultural diversity, we embark on a profound journey of understanding and connection. Culture, in its myriad forms, acts as the vibrant mural where human experiences are depicted. It encompasses the beliefs, traditions, customs, and values that shape the identities of individuals and communities across the globe. From the rich works of art from ancient civilizations to the dynamic expressions of contemporary societies, culture manifests in countless ways, each reflecting the unique essence of its creators.

Exploring the concept of culture unveils a kaleidoscope of perspectives and practices, revealing the intricate layers that comprise the human experience. It is a journey that invites us to immerse ourselves in the traditions of others, to witness the beauty of cultural expression, and to cultivate a deep appreciation for the diversity that enriches our world, our one and only home. From the vibrant hues of festivals to the solemn rituals of ceremony, culture infuses every aspect of human existence, shaping our interactions, beliefs, and aspirations.

Central to our exploration is the recognition of the profound significance of cultural awareness in the continued search for further understanding. In a world that is increasingly interconnected, the ability to navigate cultural differences with sensitivity and respect is essential all the while retaining a thirst for further knowledge. Cultural awareness invites us to transcend the confines of our own perspectives, to step into the shoes of others, and to embrace the complexity of human diversity with compassion and humility. It is through this lens of understanding that we begin to recognize the inherent humanity that unites us all, transcending the barriers of language, geography, and ideology.

Moreover, cultural awareness serves as a powerful catalyst for rapport, enabling us to forge deep connections with individuals from diverse backgrounds. As we strive to understand the experiences and perspectives of others, we can cultivate a profound sense of togetherness that transcends the boundaries of difference. This consideration becomes the foundation upon which meaningful relationships are built, fostering mutual respect, trust, and collaboration across cultural divides. Through genuine engagement and dialogue, we bridge the gap between cultures, forging bonds of solidarity and mutual understanding that transcend the limitations of prejudice and ignorance.

In essence, understanding cultural differences is not merely an intellectual exercise but a deeply human endeavor that calls upon us to embrace the richness and complexity of the world around us. It is a journey of discovery and exploration, inviting us to expand our horizons, broaden our perspectives, and embrace the beauty of cultural diversity with open hearts and minds. As we embark on this journey of cultural understanding, we paint upon the canvas of harmony, weaving together the threads of our shared humanity to create a tapestry of unity and compassion that spans the globe.

In the intricate mosaic of cultural exchange, stereotypes and biases loom as formidable barriers to genuine understanding and connection. These ingrained perceptions, shaped by a multitude of factors including media, upbringing, and societal norms, often serve to oversimplify and distort our perceptions of individuals and communities from diverse backgrounds. Rooted in ignorance and prejudice, stereotypes and biases perpetuate harmful narratives that not only obscure the richness and complexity of cultural diversity but also perpetuate division and inequality. As Cultural Chameleons committed to fostering authentic cross-cultural relationships, it is imperative that we confront and overcome these barriers with courage, empathy, and humility.

The first step in this voyage is to courageously confront the common stereotypes and biases that hinder cross-cultural understanding. These deeply entrenched beliefs, often ingrained from an early age, shape our perceptions of others and influence our interactions in profound ways. Whether it be the portrayal of certain ethnic groups in the media, the perpetuation of harmful stereotypes in popular culture, or the subtle biases that manifest in everyday interactions, stereotypes and biases pervade every aspect of our lives, often operating on a subconscious level. By shining a light on these hidden prejudices and acknowledging their impact, we can begin to dismantle their power and pave the way for genuine connection and understanding.

One of the most effective strategies for challenging and transcending stereotypes is through genuine interactions with individuals from diverse backgrounds. These meaningful exchanges provide opportunities to move beyond preconceived notions and engage with others as individuals, rather than as representatives of a particular group or culture. By approaching these interactions with an open mind and a willingness to listen and learn, we create space for authentic connections to flourish, transcending the limitations of stereotypes and biases. Whether it be through shared experiences, conversations, or collaborative endeavors, genuine interactions foster empathy, mutual respect, and a deeper appreciation for the unique perspectives and experiences of others.

Central to this process is the cultivation of empathy, the ability to understand and share the feelings of another. Empathy serves as a powerful antidote to the dehumanizing effects of stereotypes and biases, enabling us to see beyond surface-level differences and connect with the humanity that unites us all. By putting ourselves in the shoes of others and seeking to understand their experiences, we develop a deeper sense of compassion and understanding that transcends cultural divides. Through empathy, we come to recognize the inherent dignity and worth of every individual, regardless of their background or identity, and forge meaningful connections based on mutual respect and understanding.

Furthermore, challenging stereotypes and biases requires a commitment to self-reflection and introspection. It requires us to examine our own beliefs, attitudes, and behaviors, and to confront the ways in which we may contribute to perpetuating harmful narratives. This process of self-examination can be uncomfortable and confronting, as it requires us to confront our own prejudices and biases. However, it is only through this process of self-awareness and growth that we can begin to break free from the constraints of stereotypes and biases and cultivate a more inclusive and equitable society.

In addition to individual introspection, collective action is also essential in challenging systemic stereotypes and biases that perpetuate inequality and discrimination. This may involve advocating for policies and initiatives that promote diversity, equity, and inclusion in all areas of society, from education and employment to media representation and social services. It may also involve supporting organizations and initiatives that are working to combat stereotypes and biases and promote cross-cultural understanding and acceptance.

Ultimately, overcoming stereotypes and biases is a journey that requires commitment, courage, and humility. It requires us to confront our own prejudices and biases, to engage in genuine interactions with others, and to advocate for a more inclusive and equitable society. As cultural Cultural Chameleons, we embrace this journey with open hearts and open minds, recognizing that it is only through understanding, empathy, and compassion that we can truly transcend the barriers that divide us and build a world where diversity is celebrated and valued.

From a personal standpoint, I have found myself experiencing such inclinations to judge or assume, moments created from a predetermined mindset. During a trip to Thailand, I found myself on the island of Koh Tao, known for its diving spots and vibrant marine life yet far removed from any sort of Western infrastructure]. As part of my preparation for SCUBA training, I needed to get a medical check-up due to previous abdominal surgeries. In North America, such a requirement often involves a long wait, sometimes stretching to two or three hours, and I braced myself for a similar experience in Thailand. This anticipation was compounded by the common Western mindset that Thailand, often labeled a "third world country," would lack the medical efficiency and cleanliness found in the West.

To my surprise, the visit was nothing short of remarkable. Upon entering the clinic in my flip-flops, I received a few intent stares for having inadvertently done so, prior to stepping back outside to remove my footwear. In turn, the staff welcomed me warmly and spoke perfect English. The clinic was spotless, a stark contrast to the stereotypical perceptions often portrayed in media about healthcare in Southeast Asia. The doctor greeted me personally and conducted a thorough examination, even asking if I had any other medical concerns that needed addressing. The entire process, from the moment I walked in to when I left with a clean bill of health, took a mere 15 minutes and a colossal amount of 1.50 USD.

The efficiency and professionalism I encountered were astounding. The doctor, a middle-aged man with a calm demeanor, took the time to explain the results of my check-up, making sure I understood everything clearly. The nurse who assisted him was equally attentive, ensuring I felt comfortable throughout the visit. This level of care and attention far exceeded my expectations and made me realize how often we underestimate the quality of services in other parts of the world based on preconceived notions. This experience directly contradicted the Western stereotype of Thailand as a third world country with subpar medical services.

This experience shattered my preconceived notions about healthcare in Thailand. It highlighted the efficiency and professionalism of the medical system there, which I had not expected. Through this genuine interaction, I was able to transcend the stereotypes I held and gain a deeper appreciation for the culture and services in Thailand. It reminded me that assumptions often mask the true richness and competence present in different parts of the world. The kindness and efficiency I experienced in that small clinic on Koh Tao left a lasting impression on me, emphasizing the importance of approaching every new cultural encounter with an open mind and a willingness to learn.

More recently, I traveled to Eastern Europe, a region often misunderstood and stereotyped by the West. Popular perceptions depict the people as cold and the environment as bleak, with grey, uninspiring architecture. However, my experience was vastly different and eye-opening.

Upon arriving, I found the people to be incredibly warm and accommodating, proud of their rich cultural heritage. The architecture, adorned with vibrant colors, showcased incredible human feats of construction and history. Structures that seemed plain at first glance revealed intricate details and stories that spanned centuries, illustrating a deep connection to the past. The blend of old-world charm with modern innovation was nothing short of inspiring, and I was constantly in awe of the beauty hidden in every corner.

Contrary to the belief that Eastern Europe is dangerous or rough, I discovered cities that were remarkably clean and orderly. For instance, during my stay in Warsaw, the only police presence I noticed was a brief moment when officers calmly escorted an inebriated German tourist to sober up. The infrastructure was pristine and efficient, with public transportation running on time and everything being incredibly affordable. Walking through the streets, I felt a sense of safety and community, with locals going out of their way to help me navigate and share stories about their city.

The culinary experiences alone were a revelation. I indulged in hearty, traditional dishes that were both comforting and delicious, from pierogis in Poland to goulash in Hungary. Each meal was a celebration of local ingredients and culinary traditions, often shared in vibrant markets or cozy family-run restaurants. The warmth and hospitality extended to me during these meals were overwhelming, leaving me with lasting memories and a deep appreciation for the region's cultural richness.

These encounters in Thailand and Eastern Europe taught me the importance of confronting and overcoming stereotypes and biases. By engaging with people from diverse backgrounds and immersing myself in their cultures, I learned to appreciate the complexity and richness of their experiences. These personal stories emphasize the necessity of genuine interactions and open-mindedness in fostering mutual respect and a deeper understanding of the world around us. Through these journeys, I discovered that true cultural understanding goes beyond surface-level interactions and requires a genuine willingness to see and embrace the beauty in every corner of our diverse world.

However, try as you may, such matters do not always go according to plan. As I stepped into the vibrant chaos of Sao Paulo, the anticipation for the 2014 World Cup electrified the air, infusing every street corner with an infectious energy. Accompanied by my longtime friend, Mr. Rose, our shared excitement mirrored the bustling enthusiasm of the Brazilian locals, united in their passion for "futbol." Flags waved, languages intermingled, and the scent of churrasco filled the bustling streets, creating a kaleidoscope of cultural diversity that was both exhilarating and enchanting.

Navigating through the sea of humanity towards the fan area, we reveled in the chaotic beauty of the moment, checking off bucket list items with each step. The opening match of the tournament ignited the city in a frenzy of celebration, as Brazil scored their first goal, sending the crowd into a euphoric frenzy. However, amidst the jubilation, a sobering moment shattered the illusion of universal camaraderie.

In the midst of the revelry as we ran towards the stage, a sudden altercation caught my eye as Mr. Rose was forcefully thrown to the ground by police officers. Reacting instinctively, I rushed to his aid, confronting the officers who seemed poised to escalate the situation with their batons. As emotions ran high, Mr. Rose's calm demeanor and wise counsel diffused the tension from his backside, urging me to let go of my anger and move away from the escalating conflict.

In the aftermath of the incident, he shared a sobering truth about the realities of cultural dynamics in Brazil, where moments of collective euphoria often attract opportunistic individuals from marginalized communities (who were of the same color of skin) seeking to exploit the chaos. It was a stark reminder that while we may enter new environments with open minds and hearts, the complexities of cultural interaction extend beyond our idealized perceptions.

This experience served as a poignant lesson in humility and cultural sensitivity, challenging my preconceived notions and reminding me of the importance of navigating unfamiliar territories with both curiosity but awareness. In a world brimming with diversity, true cultural understanding requires not only an open mind but also a willingness to confront the uncomfortable realities that lie beneath the surface.

At the heart of our quest to navigate the intricate terrain of cultural diversity lies the pillar cultural competence. This essential quality serves as a guiding light, illuminating the path towards genuine understanding, connection, and collaboration across cultural divides. As cultural Cultural Chameleons committed to fostering meaningful cross-cultural relationships, it is paramount that we cultivate such skills with intentionality and care, recognizing their transformative power in bridging the gaps that separate us and building bridges of understanding that span the globe.

Empathy, the ability to understand and share the feelings of another, lies at the core of our capacity to connect with individuals from diverse backgrounds. It serves as a bridge that transcends the boundaries of language, geography, and culture, enabling us to forge deep and meaningful connections based on mutual understanding and respect. By putting ourselves in the shoes of others and seeking to understand their experiences, we cultivate a profound sense of compassion and empathy that serves as the foundation for genuine cross-cultural relationships.

Central to the cultivation of empathy is the practice of active listening. This involves not only hearing the words that are spoken but also paying attention to the emotions, perspectives, and cultural nuances that underlie them. By listening with an open mind and a compassionate heart, we create space for others to share their stories, experiences, and perspectives, fostering a sense of validation and understanding that transcends cultural barriers. Additionally, empathy requires us to set aside our own preconceptions and biases, allowing ourselves to truly connect with others on a deeper, more authentic level.

In addition to empathy, the cultivation of cultural competence is essential in navigating the complexities of cultural diversity with sensitivity and respect. Cultural competence refers to the ability to effectively interact with individuals from diverse cultural backgrounds and to navigate cultural differences with skill and understanding. It involves not only knowledge of cultural practices and norms but also the ability to adapt one's behavior and communication style in accordance with the cultural context.

One practical tip for developing cultural competence is to engage in continuous learning and self-reflection. This involves actively seeking out opportunities to expand your knowledge of different cultures, whether through reading, attending cultural events, or engaging in cross-cultural dialogue. By staying curious and open-minded, you can deepen your understanding of the cultural nuances that shape human interactions and cultivate a greater sense of cultural sensitivity and awareness.

Another important aspect of cultural competence is the ability to communicate effectively across cultural boundaries. This involves not only language proficiency but also an understanding of cultural communication styles, norms, and etiquette. By learning to adapt your communication style to suit the cultural context, you can avoid misunderstandings and build rapport with individuals from diverse backgrounds. Such capacities are highly sought after from a professional standpoint if not only a profoundly enriching one personally.

Additionally, developing cultural competence requires a willingness to step outside of your comfort zone and engage with individuals from diverse backgrounds in meaningful ways. This may involve seeking out opportunities to collaborate on projects, participate in cultural exchange programs, or volunteer with organizations that serve diverse communities. By actively engaging with individuals from different cultural backgrounds, you can expand your cultural competence and develop the skills and insights needed to navigate the complexities of cultural diversity with confidence and sensitivity.

Furthermore, building cultural competence involves a commitment to humility and respect. It requires us to recognize that cultural competence is a journey, not a destination, and that we must approach each interaction with a willingness to learn. By acknowledging our own limitations and embracing the diversity of human experience with curiosity, we can cultivate a deeper understanding of cultural differences and forge meaningful connections that transcend the boundaries of language, geography, and ideology.

By cultivating these qualities with intentionality and care, we can bridge the gaps that separate us, build bridges of empathy and understanding, and create a world where diversity is celebrated and valued. As cultural Cultural Chameleons, we embrace the journey of cultural competence with open hearts and open minds, recognizing that it is only through empathy, understanding, and mutual respect that we can truly build a more inclusive and equitable society.

"No one is born hating another person because of the color of his skin, or his background, or his religion. People must learn to hate, and if they can learn to hate, they can be taught to love." - Nelson Mandela[4]

---

[4] *A quote from Long Walk to Freedom.* (n.d.). https://www.goodreads.com/quo tes/111810-no-one-is-born-hating-another-person-because-of-the

4

Shockwaves and Serenity - Depths of Culture Shock

As cultural Cultural Chameleons, embarking on a journey of cultural immersion requires more than just physical preparation; it necessitates a deliberate and conscious effort to ready ourselves mentally and emotionally for the enriching experiences that lie ahead. Just as a skilled traveler meticulously plans their itinerary, we must also equip ourselves with strategies to navigate the labyrinth of cultural intricacies awaiting us. Our journey begins with a profound acknowledgment: the significance of mental and emotional preparedness in shaping our encounters with diverse cultures.

Preparing for cultural immersion demands a shift in perspective, an openness to embrace the unfamiliar and the unknown with a sense of wonder rather than trepidation. It requires us to shed the confines of our cultural comfort zones and adopt a mindset of receptivity, allowing ourselves to be permeated by the myriad of experiences that await. This mental preparedness serves as our compass, guiding us through the complexities of of future, and at times, trying encounters with poise and confidence.

To embark on this alchemic journey, it is essential to arm ourselves with an arsenal of strategies designed to cultivate mental fortitude and emotional stamina. One such strategy involves cultivating a sense of cultural curiosity, a genuine desire to learn and understand the customs, traditions, and values of the communities we are about to encounter. By approaching cultural immersion with an open heart and an inquisitive mind, we lay the foundation for authentic interactions with individuals who will contribute to this formative experience.

In addition to nurturing such emotions, thorough research is indispensable in preparing for cultural immersion. Just as a seasoned explorer meticulously maps out their route, we must diligently gather insights into the customs, traditions, and social norms of the destinations we intend to visit. Through meticulous research, we gain invaluable insights into the cultural quilt of our host communities, enabling us to navigate their intricacies with detail and respect. From understanding the significance of cultural rituals to familiarizing ourselves with local etiquette, each piece of knowledge acquired serves as a stepping stone towards cultural fluency and mutual understanding.

Yet, preparation extends beyond mere intellectual understanding, it encompasses a holistic approach to emotional readiness as well. As we venture into unfamiliar territory, we must acknowledge the inevitability of encountering moments of discomfort and disorientation. However, rather than viewing these moments as obstacles, we can reframe them as opportunities for growth and self-discovery. By embracing the inherent challenges of cultural immersion with optimism and stoic thought, we empower ourselves to navigate the depths of culture shock with tranquility and equanimity.

In essence, preparing for cultural immersion is a multifaceted endeavor that demands both intellectual curiosity and emotional conditioning. By cultivating a sense of cultural curiosity and arming ourselves with knowledge, we lay the groundwork for meaningful cross-cultural exchanges. Moreover, by embracing the challenges of cultural immersion with an open heart, we position ourselves to navigate the complexities of cultural encounters with grace and serenity. As cultural Cultural Chameleons, our journey begins not with the physical act of travel, but with the profound transformation that occurs within ourselves as we embark on the next adventure of our inquisitive life.

During such odysseys, traversing the diverse landscapes of global cultures, we inevitably encounter the phenomenon known as culture shock, a seismic shift in our perceptions and emotions as we navigate unfamiliar cultural terrain. Like a turbulent sea, culture shock can engulf us in a whirlwind of emotions, challenging our sense of identity and belonging. Yet, amidst the tumultuous waves, there exists a pathway to serenity, a task of self-discovery that enables us to not only survive but thrive in the face of cultural disorientation.

Embarking on my journey to India, a land so vibrant and

diverse that it defies simple explanation, I felt prepared for the adventure ahead. With numerous stamps in my passport and a wealth of travel experiences under my belt, I considered myself a seasoned explorer, ready to immerse myself in the rich tapestry of Indian culture. However, nothing could have prepared me for the sheer magnitude of the culture shock that awaited me.

From the tranquil foothills of the Himalayas to the bustling streets of New Delhi, India greeted me with a sensory overload unlike anything I had ever experienced. The cacophony of sounds, the riot of colors, and the exotic scents that filled the air left me simultaneously exhilarated and disoriented. As I navigated through crowded markets where vendors hawked their wares and stray animals roamed freely, I found myself questioning my ability to adapt to this new and unfamiliar environment.

One particularly vivid memory stands out in my mind: the moment I unwittingly stepped over a deceased individual lying on the sidewalk. It was a stark reminder of the harsh realities of life in a country where poverty and overcrowding are ever-present.

Traveling with two female companions, we found ourselves the recipients of both curious stares and acts that left us astonished and, at times, deeply uncomfortable. From strangers placing their infants in our laps for photo ops to children eagerly interacting with us while subtly seeking compensation, it was clear that our presence as foreigners generated a mix of fascination and opportunism. One particularly unsettling experience occurred at the Red Fort, where a group of young men followed us persistently, making us feel increasingly uneasy.

The situation escalated further in the airport customs line. As we waited, a grown man attempted to circumvent my cylindrical tapestry carrying case to rub up against the girls I was with. In a moment of instinctive protectiveness, I grabbed him by the ear and pulled him away. This shocking and disrespectful behavior was swiftly addressed by a nearby customs agent, who had observed the entire incident. The agent assured me he would handle the man and emphasized that such conduct was unacceptable, reinforcing that, regardless of where one is in the world, respecting others' personal space is paramount.

These experiences served as stark reminders that, despite our best preparations and travel experiences, we can still encounter unexpected and challenging situations. The cultural shock of such blatant disrespect was a sobering reminder of the complexities and unpredictabilities of navigating new environments. However, these moments also highlighted the importance of standing up against inappropriate behavior and the crucial role of local authorities in maintaining order and respect.

Reflecting on my experiences in India, I realized that no amount of preparation could have fully shielded me from the shock of encountering a culture so vastly different from my own. Yet, it was precisely this shock that served as a catalyst for personal growth and self-discovery. In the end, I emerged from my journey not only with a newfound appreciation of the incredibly wide spectrum of Indian culture but also with a deeper understanding of the world around me.

This understanding deepened further during my travels in Colombia, a country rich in history and cultural vibrancy. Upon arrival in Cartagena, I was immediately struck by the throngs of vendors aggressively vying for the attention of tourists. It was impossible to walk along the beach, have a conversation, or even sit down without being approached by merchants selling everything from trinkets to unsolicited massages. One particularly memorable incident occurred when a stranger began massaging my shoulders without consent. I had to forcefully stand up, grab their arms, and firmly state in Spanish, "No necesito absolutamente nada" ("I absolutely don't need anything").

Leaving Cartagena, I felt rattled but remained aware that Colombia was still experiencing its own set of challenges. My request for tinted windows in my rental car was a precautionary measure as I drove down the coast past Barranquilla. The journey was punctuated by a heavily armed military checkpoint, which was both a reminder of the region's tumultuous past and a harbinger of the stark contrasts to come. Just ten kilometers past the checkpoint, I found myself in a small, impoverished pueblo, surrounded by serrated aluminum homes and heaps of garbage. To my fellow traveler's fright, a young boy, no older than fourteen, wandered barefoot through the trash with an AK47 slung over his shoulder.

Internally, I used humor to calm my nerves, wondering what the boy might be hunting with such a weapon. Yet, the reality was clear: breaking down in this area would not be ideal. However, after hours of driving, we finally arrived in Santa Marta, where the warmth and hospitality of our hosts awaited us. As we toured the city and watched a distant storm from the beach, I had time to reflect. Despite the hardships and the moments of fear, I recognized that the people we encountered were, like us, simply trying to navigate their lives. This realization brought a profound sense of empathy and understanding, allowing me to sleep soundly that night.

These experiences underscored the unpredictable nature of culture shock and its potential to teach us invaluable life lessons. Despite extensive preparation and a wealth of travel experience, each new destination brought its own unique challenges and surprises. Embracing these moments with an open heart and mind not only enriched my journey but also transformed my perspective. Traveling and seeking such experiences continues to be a powerful teacher, reminding me that the world is vast, diverse, and full of opportunities for growth. Each encounter, whether disorienting or enlightening, contributes to a deeper understanding of humanity and my place within it.

Embracing culture shock necessitates a deep understanding of its stages and the adoption of coping mechanisms tailored to each phase. By recognizing the signs and symptoms of culture shock, we can effectively navigate its tumultuous waters and emerge stronger and more resilient on the other side.

The first stage of culture shock is often characterized by feelings of euphoria and excitement, a honeymoon period during which everything seems new and enchanting. Yet, beneath the surface lies a sense of disorientation as we grapple with the unfamiliarity of our surroundings. It is during this initial phase that we may find ourselves experiencing a range of emotions, from exhilaration to apprehension, as we navigate the complexities of cultural adjustment.

As the honeymoon phase fades, we enter the second stage of culture shock, the onset of frustration and disillusionment. Suddenly, the novelty of our surroundings gives way to the harsh realities of cultural differences, leaving us feeling overwhelmed and out of place. It is during this phase that we may experience a sense of homesickness or longing for the familiarity of our own culture, a longing that can manifest itself in feelings of isolation and alienation.

The third stage of culture shock is perhaps the most challenging, a period of adjustment and acceptance. As we gradually acclimate to our new cultural environment, we begin to develop coping mechanisms to navigate its complexities with greater ease. Yet, despite our efforts to adapt, we may still encounter moments of frustration and misunderstanding as we strive to find our place in this unfamiliar landscape.

Finally, as we emerge from the depths of culture shock, we enter the fourth stage - a phase of acceptance and integration. Here, we find peace amidst the chaos, embracing the cultural differences that once seemed insurmountable with a sense of grace and humility. It is during this phase that we truly come to appreciate the beauty of cultural diversity, recognizing that it is through our differences that we find our greatest strength.

To cope with the challenges of culture shock, it is essential to adopt strategies that promote self-awareness and well-being at each stage of the journey. In the initial stages of culture shock, maintaining a positive mindset is paramount. By focusing on the opportunities for growth and discovery that your current state presents, we can cultivate a sense of optimism that carries us through the inevitable challenges ahead.

Moreover, seeking out social support can be invaluable in coping with culture shock. Whether through connecting with fellow travelers or engaging with members of the local community, building a support network can provide us with the encouragement and reassurance we need to navigate the complexities of cultural adjustment.

In addition to fostering a positive mindset and seeking social support, practicing self-care is essential in coping with culture shock. Taking time to engage in activities that nourish our mind, body, and spirit can help alleviate stress and promote emotional well-being. Whether through meditation, exercise, or creative expression, prioritizing self-care enables us to maintain a sense of balance and resilience amidst the challenges of cultural immersion.

In the intricate depths of cultural immersion, adaptation is the thread that binds us to our surroundings, enabling us to navigate the intricate web of social norms and customs with grace and humility. As Cultural Chameleons, our ability to accept new environments and embrace the diversity of cultural differences is paramount to our success and fulfillment on our journey.

Practical techniques for versatility are essential tools in our cultural toolkit, empowering us to navigate the complexities of cultural immersion with confidence and serenity. From mastering the art of nonverbal communication to understanding the nuances of local etiquette, these techniques provide us with the necessary skills to thrive in any cultural environment.

Moreover, developing effective communication skills is essential for new environments and social norms. Whether through verbal or nonverbal communication, our ability to express ourselves clearly and respectfully is key to building meaningful connections and fostering mutual understanding. By actively listening to others and being mindful of our own communication style, we can bridge cultural divides and cultivate harmonious relationships with individuals from diverse backgrounds.

Ultimately, the key to successful adaptation lies in our willingness to learn from cultural differences, without shying away from the potential for discomfort. To approach each encounter with humility yet confidence, eager to glean insights and perspectives that broaden our horizons and enrich our lives.

As we embark on our travels seeking certain emotional depths in faraway lands, we arm ourselves with strategies for success, essential tools in our cultural toolkit. From cultivating awareness to mastering effective communication skills, these techniques empower us to navigate the complexities of such experiences and in turn everyday obstacles. By remaining nimble, versatile, and open-minded, we not only adapt to new environments and social norms but also embrace the inevitable culture shock as a transformative experience. It is in these unfamiliar territories, away from the comforts of our known homes, that we find opportunities for profound learning and growth. Through perseverance and an unwavering spirit of exploration, we forge meaningful connections, fostering mutual understanding and leaving a lasting impact on both ourselves and the cultures we encounter.

"Culture shock is the revelation that there are as many ways of being human as there are people on this earth." - Khaled Hosseini, The Kite Runner[5]

---

[5] Hosseini, K. (2011). *The Kite Runner: Rejacketed*. A&C Black.

5

Rhythms of Resonance - The Local Lens

Engaging with local communities is akin to tuning into the vibrant melodies of a foreign everyday life, each with its unique cadence and rhythm. In the symphony of global diversity, these encounters serve as pivotal moments of transformation, enriching our understanding of the world and ourselves. As Cultural Chameleons chameleons, we recognize the profound value in immersing ourselves in the daily rhythms of communities far and wide, embracing the opportunity to learn, grow, and evolve.

At the heart of our journey lies the profound significance of learning from local communities. These encounters offer more than mere observation; they invite us to actively participate in the intricate dance of daily life, immersing ourselves in the rich educational opportunity of traditions, customs, and beliefs. Through this immersive experience, we gain invaluable insights into the essence of a culture, transcending surface-level observations to uncover the deeper truths that shape its identity.

One of the most transcendent aspects of engaging with local communities is the opportunity to witness life through their lens. By stepping into their world, we shed preconceived notions and open ourselves to new perspectives, challenging our assumptions and broadening our horizons. Whether it's sharing a meal with a family in a remote village or participating in traditional ceremonies, these immersive experiences offer profound lessons that reshape our worldview and ignite a sense of empathy and understanding.

Consider, for instance, my paradigm-shifting trek to the mountains of Northern India. Venturing beyond the tourist trails, I immersed myself in the daily lives of the local Buddhist community. Spending time in a Himalayan monastery, I lived in the chambers of a 2,000-year-old monastery. Walking the steps was initially a challenge at 4,000 meters of altitude, but the experience was profoundly enriching. I had the opportunity to teach young monks lessons in geography, English, and French. I had never seen such an intent to learn, as they were simply happy with the opportunity for education.

One of the most touching moments was meeting a child, now an adolescent, whom I had sponsored for a decade. He explained to me what his everyday life was like and thanked me for his opportunities. It must have been dusty that day as my eyes watered. Additionally, I spent time in a home with some villagers, where my efforts had provided their youngest son with the opportunity for schooling. I was generally unable to move in their home as their hugs were given in perpetuity.

On one memorable evening, I received a dinner invite, and to my surprise, the entire village showed up. Unbeknownst to me, the guest eats before everyone else. Roughly 25 people were stacked into a small home, all intently watching me digest what was more a trough than a plate of momos (dumplings). And as we all know, in every corner of the globe, we like to poke fun at each other. My Lama guide called my name, and unknowingly, I looked. Well, if you look left when eating there, they fill your plate again. I looked back to see the very same volume with which I had begun. As everyone nodded yes, I heavily nodded no, ringing the bell of defeat. I've never been so full.

The next morning, while contemplating and smiling about current events, I immersed myself in one of my favorite parts of this small community—washing my clothes on a rock with a basin as the sun rose over the Himalayas. These were moments of clarity that I still find difficult to quantify, though they are moments I wish for each and every one of you.

My jaunt to Cuba was a moment where I was able to share in an immersion in local culture with those close to me. Cuba, a wonderful place where the warmth and kindness of the people greatly underscore the poverty and lack of resources many live with due to decades of embargoes. Visiting Cuba is like stepping into a time warp, with old cars and machinery from the 1950s and 60s still in use. While most North Americans, including my travel partners, were content to stay in the resorts with their free-flowing poorly mixed drinks and mystery meat buffets, I felt a pull to experience more of the local scene.

I had brought a suitcase full of belongings to donate, and

as a rule of thumb, I always speak with the staff—cleaning, concierge, and others. One of the valets offered an introduction to his cousin for an evening outing. After some convincing, my friends and I met up with a gentleman named Denis, who turned out to have a pristine 1960 Pontiac Bonneville. He drove us to a family home where we met several generations living under one roof.

The "abuela" was clearly in charge, and I helped translate in my broken Spanish as she shared stories from the pre-communist era to the present day. We heard tales of hardship and struggle due to the US embargo, as well as the ingenious games the kids had created to pass the time. Despite the difficulties, there was an undeniable spirit of resilience and joy in the family.

We were treated to an incredible barbecue with cold beers, music, and, to my friends' amusement, my clumsy attempts at salsa dancing. The generosity and warmth of our hosts left a lasting impression on us all. My friends still talk about the smiles they remember and the hospitality they experienced that night.

These moments of connection and cultural exchange highlight the wonders that await when you step off the beaten path and leave the large resorts behind. Embrace the opportunity to immerse yourself in local communities, and you will discover a richness of experience that no resort can offer. Get out of your comfort zone and seek the local experience, you won't regret it.

These anecdotes illuminate the effect of engaging with local communities, reminding us of the profound wisdom that resides in the hearts and minds of people around the world. Whether it's gaining insight into age-old traditions or forging meaningful connections with individuals from diverse backgrounds, these encounters serve as catalysts for personal growth and cultural exchange. We embrace the opportunity to harmonize with the rhythms of diverse cultures, recognizing that in the symphony of global diversity, every voice adds a unique and beautiful melody to the chorus of humanity.

At the heart of cross-cultural communication lies a profound appreciation for the subtleties that shape our interactions. Unlike the simplicity of linguistic translation, effective communication across cultural boundaries requires a deep understanding of context, subtext, and cultural cues. Every gesture, tone, and expression carries layers of meaning, shaping the dynamics of our interactions and influencing the outcomes of our conversations. As wanderers of intent, we recognize the importance of decoding these subtleties, honing our sensitivity to cultural nuances, and embracing the complexities of intercultural communication.

Language barriers, though formidable, are but one facet of the intricate mosaic of cross-cultural communication. Beyond mere words lies a vast landscape of cultural differences, each presenting its own set of challenges and opportunities. From the intricacies of nonverbal communication to the subtleties of social etiquette, navigating these cultural nuances requires a blend of patience, curiosity, and humility. By immersing ourselves in the cultural context of our interactions, we gain a deeper understanding of the people we seek to connect with, transcending linguistic barriers to forge meaningful connections based on empathy and mutual respect.

At the heart of our quest for common ground lies a deep appreciation for the universal aspects of humanity that connect us across cultures. From the primal emotions of joy and sorrow to the fundamental need for belonging and connection, these shared experiences form the foundation of our shared humanity, serving as touchstones that resonate across time and space. As cultural Cultural Chameleons, we seek to amplify these universal truths, celebrating the richness of diversity while honoring the commonalities that unite us all.

"To my mind, the greatest reward and luxury of travel is to be able to experience everyday things as if for the first time." – Bill Bryson[6]

---

[6] *A quote by Bill Bryson.* (n.d.). https://www.goodreads.com/quotes/3224147-to-my-mind-the-greatest-reward-and-luxury-of-travel

6

Soulful Solutions - Infusing Passion into Problem-Solving

Adapting to unfamiliar environments is akin to embarking on a exploration of self-discovery, where each step reveals new landscapes and challenges. This voyage is not merely about luxury or sight-seeing; it's about flourishing amidst the unknown, infusing every encounter with passion and purpose. As they traverse uncharted terrains, they employ a repertoire of strategies honed through experience and intuition, seamlessly navigating the intricate web of transportation, accommodation, and daily routines.

Transportation becomes a symphony of exploration, where trains, buses, and rickshaws orchestrate the rhythm of the journey. Such travelers (not tourists) approach each mode of transport not as a mere means to an end but as an opportunity to immerse themselves in the heartbeat of the locale. They embrace the chaos of crowded stations and bustling terminals, finding solace in the shared humanity of fellow travelers like worker bees in a hive. Whether navigating the labyrinthine subway systems of metropolises or embarking on winding jungle roads, they remain agile in their approach, embracing spontaneity with open arms.

Accommodation serves as a sanctuary amidst the whirlwind of adventure, offering a haven to recharge and reflect. For Cultural Chameleons, every hotel room, hostel bunk, or homestay is not just a place to lay their heads; it's a canvas and potential for exchange and connection. They seek out accommodations that resonate with the soul of the destination, immersing themselves in the fabric of local life. From quaint guesthouses run by hospitable hosts to eco-lodges nestled in pristine wilderness, each abode becomes a chapter in their unfolding narrative, fostering bonds that transcend language and borders.

Daily routines take on a delightful hue, as one embraces the ebb and flow of life in unfamiliar surroundings. From sunrise rituals to sunset soirées, every moment becomes an opportunity to savor the essence of the destination. They relish the culinary delights of street markets and hole-in-the-wall eateries, savoring the flavors of tradition and innovation. Whether partaking in ancient rituals or modern-day festivities, they approach each experience with reverence and curiosity, enriching their understanding of their existing buoyancy in the cultural sea that envelops them.

Yet, amidst such adventures, unexpected challenges and setbacks inevitably arise, testing the resilience of even the most seasoned travelers. Coping with adversity is not merely a matter of survival; it's an opportunity to cultivate and expand on a capacity of resourcefulness. Cultural Chameleons appreciate each obstacle as a catalyst for growth, drawing upon their inner reserves of strength conditioned from previous feats of similar maneuvering. Whether navigating language barriers or uncharted territories, they approach each challenge with tenacity and grace, emerging stronger and wiser with every trial.

Arriving in Bangkok, Thailand after bidding a farewell to a dear friend in Dubai, I found myself once again swept up in the whirlwind of wanderlust. Despite the language barrier, I felt the magnetic pull of the "land of a thousand smiles", beckoning me with its promises of adventure and mystery. Adding a dash of excitement, I had opted to forgo the task of booking accommodation beforehand. Little did I know that my impromptu decision would soon become a comical anecdote in the occasional obstacles ones travels can produce.

As I faced the scrutinizing gaze of the customs agent, my fatigue-induced delirium led to a confession of my spontaneous intentions. With a bemused smile, the agent kindly suggested a suitable abode or at least an acceptable answer for my entry card, perhaps sensing the impending chaos that would ensue. And so, armed with my stamp of approval for entry into the country, I set forth into the vibrant chaos of Bangkok.

However, my attempts to secure lodging resembled a slapstick comedy, with each hotel door metaphorically slamming shut in my weary face. Frustrated and disheveled, I stumbled upon a group of Thai gentlemen engaged in lively banter amidst a sea of tuk-tuks and scooters. Desperate for a glimmer of hope (or perhaps just a cold drink), I joined their midst, instantly becoming the weary protagonist in this impromptu farce.

Despite our linguistic divide, the universal language of hospitality prevailed as my new companions welcomed me with open arms (and a cold beer, bless their souls). Amidst laughter and broken English, I regaled them with tales of my globe-trotting escapades, each story better received than the last. In a moment of serendipity, one of the men offered to play the role of my knight in shining armor, seeking out a hotel fit for royalty.

To my astonishment, the accommodation not only provided a plush bed to rest my weary bones but also came with a price tag that left me questioning whether I had stumbled into a parallel universe where luxury was the norm. As I sank into the decadent comfort of my surroundings, my thoughts turned solemn as I learned of the passing of King Bhumibol Adulyadej, the world's longest-reigning monarch.

In the midst of my whimsical misadventures, I paused to pay my respects to the Thai people, who were mourning the loss of their revered king. Despite the jovial tone of my escapades, I felt a profound sense of reverence for their culture and traditions, reminded once again of the profound beauty and complexity of the world we inhabit. And so, with a heart full of gratitude and a newfound appreciation for the kindness of strangers, and how my adaptable nature brought for solutions to the challenges set forth before me; I embarked on my next adventure, eager to uncover the treasures that awaited me in the enchanting land of Thailand.

When seeking to resolve an obstacle, the worst most people

will say is "no." I prefer to find out than wonder if. Problem-solving across cultures is a dynamic dance, where the rhythm of diverse perspectives ideally converges to create harmonious solutions. This dance is not merely a series of steps; it's an intricate interplay of creativity and collaboration. As we navigate the intricate maze of cultural differences in problem-solving approaches and decision-making processes, embrace each challenge as an opportunity to foster understanding and forge connections across borders.

Cultural differences in problem-solving approaches and decision-making processes form the colorful threads, each strand weaving its unique narrative into our own fabric of personal growth. For Cultural Chameleons, understanding these differences is the first step towards building bridges of cooperation. From the meticulous planning of Western business meetings to the fluidity of Eastern consensus-building, they approach each cultural nuance with curiosity and respect, seeking common ground by way of entertaining the diversity of perspectives.

Strategies for collaborating and finding solutions in multi-cultural contexts require a delicate balance of flexibility and sensitivity. These strategies are not just tools shaped over time; they are sharpened guiding principles that inform every interaction and decision. An approach with an open mind and a humble heart, recognizing that true understanding requires active listening and accepting that we are all at some point incorrect.

Creativity becomes the lifeblood of problem-solving, using

diverse perspectives to spark innovation and ingenuity. They recognize that creativity knows no boundaries; it flourishes in the fertile soil of cultural diversity. From blending traditional wisdom with modern technologies to adapting time-honored practices to new contexts, they approach problem-solving with a spirit of experimentation and exploration honed guided by past experiences. They embrace failure as a natural part of the creative process, learning and growing from each setback with determination.

At the end of a very long journey, I approached the coastal town of Santa Marta, Colombia, with a sense of both relief and anticipation. This trip had been riddled with harrowing moments, including insane bus drivers overtaking each other into oncoming traffic, forcing me to use the shoulder to avoid head-on collisions, and kamikaze motorcyclists merging into highway traffic from all directions. Yet, despite these challenges, I found myself captivated by the beauty of the coastal environment, particularly the two-lane passage through the "Santuario de Flora y Fauna Ciénaga Grande," with its diverse vegetation and small fishing homes on stilts.

As we neared Santa Marta, I slowed down, recognizing my responsibility to get us to our lodging for the next few days. Instinctively, I started making mental notes of different sites and areas I wanted to explore, letting my curiosity guide me. Like many travelers today, I relied on my GPS to direct me, the soothing English voice offering accessible information. However, as fate would have it, this technological guide led us astray, taking us down the literal wrong path.

After fifteen minutes of my phone recalculating and leading us deeper into the tougher parts of town, where windows were barred and doors triple-bolted, I decided to take control. I stopped the car at an intersection just as a torrential downpour began, causing the street to flood at an alarming rate. With reception dropping in and out, I darted out of the car, aware of the watchful eyes from behind the barred windows of the surrounding houses.

Opening the trunk to find an umbrella, I climbed onto the roof of the vehicle, desperately trying to enter every location I had memorized on our way into town. Finally, a hit: a Mercado right at the entrance of town, and by sheer luck, my phone briefly displayed a map. I jumped back into the car, reassuring my travel companion with a quick, "Everything is okay," and urged, "Let's do this," as water began seeping in through the doors.

With my heart pounding and the rain pouring down, I navigated through the flooding streets, relying on my memory and the brief glimpse of the map. As we finally reached the Mercado, the sense of relief was palpable. My travel companion, wide-eyed but trusting, marveled at our successful navigation through such a precarious situation. It was a testament to the importance of adaptability and resourcefulness, core traits of any true Cultural Chameleon.

Reflecting on the experience, I realized that problem-solving often involves embracing the unexpected and making the best of challenging situations. By combining traditional wisdom, like mental mapping and instinct, with modern technology,

I was able to navigate a potentially disastrous situation. This blend of old and new, along with a spirit of experimentation and the willingness to embrace failure, is what drives innovation and resilience in any context.

Exploring how diversity fosters creativity and innovation in problem-solving is a journey into the heart of human potential, where unique perspectives converge to create a symphony of innovation. For Cultural Chameleons, diversity is not just a buzzword; it's a cornerstone of their approach to problem-solving. They recognize that true innovation thrives on the anvil of pushing boundaries, where the collision of contrasting ideas sparks the fires of creativity. From multicultural teams to cross-disciplinary collaborations, they cultivate environments that celebrate diversity as a catalyst for metamorphic change, nurturing a culture of innovation that knows no bounds.

My own journey through the challenges of navigating Santa Marta is a testament to the power of diverse perspectives and resourcefulness. Faced with a daunting obstacle, I relied on a combination of instinct, cultural awareness, and modern technology to find a solution. This blend of traditional wisdom and nimble thinking is what enables Cultural Chameleons to thrive in any environment, turning potential setbacks into stories shared around the dinner table.

As I reflect on the experience, I am reminded of the importance of approaching problem-solving with an open mind and a humble heart. True understanding requires active listening and a willingness to admit when we are wrong. By embracing the array of cultural diversity, we can unlock new ways of thinking and create solutions that are both innovative and inclusive. The journey through Santa Marta was more than just a logistical challenge; it was a vivid example of how embracing the unknown and adapting to new circumstances can lead to profound insights and meaningful connections.

In the face of adversity, the ability to draw upon diverse perspectives and experiences becomes a powerful tool. The people I encountered, from the customs agent in Bangkok to the helpful strangers who openly shared their tasty cold beverages, each contributed to my journey in ways that were both unexpected and invaluable. These encounters highlight the importance of empathy and collaboration in navigating the complexities of our world. By fostering an environment where voices are heard and every perspective is valued, we can create a more inclusive and innovative future.

Ultimately, such experiences of around the world underscore the innate power of diversity. Whether it's blending traditional wisdom with modern technologies, or adapting time-honored practices to new contexts, the key to effective problem-solving lies in our ability to embrace change and learn from each other. As we continue to explore the limitless potential of human creativity, we must remember that it is our shared experiences and diverse perspectives that light the way forward, guiding us toward a more harmonious world.

"In the middle of difficulty lies opportunity." – Albert Einstein[7]

---

[7] A quote by Albert Einstein. (n.d.). https://www.goodreads.com/quotes/727 5-in-the-middle-of-difficulty-lies-opportunity

7

Blooms in the Desert - Thriving When Lost in Translation

In the vast landscape of human interactions, one of the most daunting challenges that cultural Cultural Chameleons encounter is navigating through the labyrinth of rejection and misunderstandings. As we traverse these uncharted territories, we inevitably face moments of conflict and confusion, where our words may fall on deaf ears or our actions may be misinterpreted. It is in these moments that our fluidity and robustness are put to the test, as we strive to find common ground enveloping a diversity of perspectives and expectations.

Managing conflicts and misunderstandings in all interactions requires a balance empathy, communication, and ideally, previous levels of competence. One of the fundamental strategies for overcoming these obstacles is to approach each interaction with an open mind and a willingness to learn. Aristotle, the ancient Greek philosopher, known for his works on subjects of logic and ethics, so accurately expressed: "It is the mark of

59

an educated mind to be able to entertain a thought without accepting it."[8] Acknowledging and respecting the cultural differences between ourselves and others, we can foster mutual understanding and appreciation that transcends linguistic and social barriers. Moreover, actively listening to the perspectives and concerns of others can help mitigate conflicts before they escalate, allowing for more meaningful and constructive dialogue.

However, even with the best intentions and communication skills, rejection and a perception of insensitivity may still arise in our interactions. In these moments, it is essential to return to the chameleonic traits one has worked on from previous challenges, the ability to bounce back from setbacks and adapt to changing circumstances. Rather than dwelling on past rejections or allowing ourselves to be consumed by negative emotions, we can choose to view these experiences as opportunities for growth and self-improvement. By reframing rejection as a natural part of the learning process, we can develop a more positive and proactive mindset that empowers us to persevere in the face of adversity.

One effective strategy for cultivating grit in the face of rejection is to focus on building strong support networks from individuals who have navigated similar challenges in the past. By surrounding ourselves with positive influences and role models, we can gain valuable insights and perspectives that help us navigate difficult times with greater confidence and determination. Additionally, practicing self-care and mindfulness techniques

---

[8]   M.Kumar. (2008). *Dictionary of Quotations.* APH Publishing.

can help mitigate the negative effects of rejection on our mental and emotional well-being, allowing us to maintain a sense of balance and perspective even in the midst of the hurdles life can put forth.

Ultimately, the key to thriving when lost in translation lies in our ability to adapt and persevere in the face of rejection and misunderstandings, it is not the tallest tree or the brightest flower that survives, but rather the one that can bend and sway with the shifting sands of change, blooming brightly amidst the chaos and confusion.

Strolling the streets of my favorite metropolis in the world, I found myself somewhat lost in Tokyo, perhaps on purpose. A city that effortlessly encompasses the wide spectrum from complete serenity to utter pandemonium, Tokyo is a place where getting lost feels like a grand adventure. I was solo on this journey, armed with the twenty words of Japanese I believed I understood and could ideally speak.

This day had been one of exploration by intentionally getting lost in the multiple alleys that spider out from any given intersection and then attempting to retrace my steps. During my excursion, I made an interesting observation: in many shops, when I asked a question, the cashier would knock on a small door that led to a room where someone else was working. It seemed that the man behind the small door next to the cash always held the answer.

Later that day, after enjoying some spicy ramen from my favorite Japanese lady, who perfected my dish with such care and intent that it embodied the intoxicating spirit of Japanese culture, I began my search for the Robot Restaurant. A recommendation from a fellow world enthusiast and Tokyo veteran[9], was situated in the massive red-light district of Kabukichō—a sea of lights, sounds, and humanity that set all my senses on fire.

In a bewildered state with my entrance time quickly approaching, I started to stop passersby to ask for directions. In a moment of complete surprise, I attempted to stop an older gentleman and perhaps, in my haste, startled him or nudged him without any intent to harm, of course. The offense in this interaction was palpable. His anger continued to escalate as a younger man ran up and began to aggressively wave me away, using words I can only imagine were not of kindness. I left feeling a bit shocked and somewhat saddened because it is never my intent to offend. What had I done to cause such a commotion?

Fortunately, others who had seen this event unfold approached me. When I showed my ticket with some hesitation, I was immediately greeted with smiles, and a group of adolescents kindly walked me to the entrance of the Robot Restaurant. While I enjoyed wave after wave of ornate floats, large dancing robots, and incredible acrobats in a large underground stadium with a cold beer and an incredible bento box, my mind kept returning to the earlier incident.

It eventually dawned on me that I had breached several basic

---

[9]   https://www.reformatt.com/ - Matthijs van Vuuren

concepts of Japanese culture. First and foremost, respecting your elders is deeply ingrained in Japanese society. My inadvertent jostling of the older gentleman was a significant breach of this custom. Secondly, physical contact, especially with strangers, is generally avoided in Japan unless it is explicitly invited. My hurried attempt to stop him must have felt intrusive and disrespectful. Thirdly, proper greetings are paramount in Japanese interactions. A simple bow, a polite salute, or even an "excuse me" in Japanese would have been a better approach, reflecting the respect and humility expected in such encounters.

Realizing my mistakes, I felt a mix of embarrassment and determination. I didn't want this misunderstanding to overshadow my experience. With this newfound understanding of cultural nuances, I resolved to navigate my interactions more thoughtfully. This determination led me to an impromptu decision. I decided to visit the Park Hyatt in Shinjuku, the iconic setting of one of my favorite films, "Lost in Translation."[10] The irony of the title wasn't lost on me; it seemed a fitting destination for the day's lessons.

Talking my way into the Park Hyatt was a blend of confidence and newfound cultural sensitivity. I approached the concierge with a respectful bow and politely inquired if I could have a look around, mentioning my admiration for the film. To my delight, they graciously allowed me to explore. As I ascended to the New York Bar on the top floor, I marveled at the stunning panoramic views of Tokyo. The city lights stretched endlessly, a mesmerizing sea of twinkling brilliance against the night sky.

---

[10] King, G. (2010b). *Lost in translation*. Edinburgh University Press.

Sipping a perfectly crafted cocktail in the ambiance of the bar, I reflected on the day's events. The mix of modern elegance and cultural depth of the Park Hyatt seemed to encapsulate the essence of Tokyo itself. It was a city where tradition and innovation coexisted harmoniously, and I felt grateful for the opportunity to learn and grow from my experiences. My missteps had taught me invaluable lessons about cultural sensitivity and the importance of adapting to the nuances of each place I visited.

In the vast landscape of everyday interactions, there exists an oasis of growth and transformation for those brave enough to venture beyond the familiar shores of comfort. It is here, amidst the swirling sands of discomfort and uncertainty, that Cultural Chameleons discover the true extent of their dexterity and determination. For it is in these moments of vulnerability and unease that we are presented with the greatest opportunities for growth and self-assessment, as we learn to embrace discomfort as a catalyst for change and transformation.

Stepping outside one's comfort zone is not merely an act of bravery but a fundamental prerequisite for true growth and self-discovery. By pushing ourselves beyond the boundaries of what is familiar and routine, we open ourselves up to new experiences and perspectives that have the power to challenge and reshape our understanding of the world. Whether it be immersing ourselves in a foreign culture, learning a new language, or taking on a challenging project, each step outside our comfort zone serves as a catalyst for our evolution.

The transformative power of embracing discomfort lies in its ability to push us beyond our perceived limitations. When we willingly expose ourselves to situations that evoke feelings of uncertainty or unease, we create opportunities for self-improvement that would otherwise remain undiscovered. Rather than shying away from discomfort, let us learn to lean into it, recognizing it as a sign of progress and evolution on the path toward personal and professional fulfillment.

In the arid terrain of cross-cultural interactions, resilience and perseverance stand as towering monuments to the human spirit, testaments to the indomitable will of those who refuse to be defined by the barriers they face. It is here, amidst the harsh winds of adversity and uncertainty, that Cultural Chameleons demonstrate the true depth of their adaptability and fortitude, rising above the challenges that threaten to derail their journey towards personal and professional fulfillment.

Exploring the resilience of cultural pioneers reveals a common thread that binds them together: a steadfast commitment to their goals and a willingness to persevere in the face of adversity. Whether they are navigating language barriers, cultural norms, or systemic discrimination, these individuals refuse to be deterred by the challenges that lie ahead. Instead, they draw upon their inner strength and resilience to overcome obstacles with grace and determination, emerging stronger and more resilient with each passing trial.

Strategies for building resilience and perseverance in navigating diverse environments are as varied and unique as the individuals who employ them. One such strategy is the cultivation of a growth mindset, which emphasizes the belief that intelligence and abilities can be developed through dedication and hard work. By adopting a growth mindset,we can view challenges as opportunities for learning and growth, rather than insurmountable barriers to success.

Additionally, seeking out mentorship and support from individuals who have successfully navigated similar challenges can provide invaluable guidance and encouragement along the journey. By surrounding themselves with positive influences and role models, Cultural Chameleons can gain valuable insights and perspectives that help them navigate difficult times with greater confidence and determination. Moreover, by building strong support networks and fostering meaningful connections with others, they can draw upon the collective wisdom and strength of their community to overcome obstacles and achieve their goals.

In the desert of cross-cultural interactions, where the sands of adversity and uncertainty threaten to engulf even the most determined of travelers, resilience and perseverance serve as guiding lights, leading cultural chameleons toward their destination with unwavering resolve. By exploring the resilience of individuals who have overcome cultural barriers and adopting strategies for building resilience and perseverance in navigating diverse environments, cultural chameleons can unlock the full potential of their adaptability and fortitude, blooming brightly amidst the chaos and confusion. For it is in the moments of greatest adversity that we discover the true depth of our strength and resilience, emerging stronger, wiser, and more resilient than ever before.

"Translation is not a matter of words only: it is a matter of

making intelligible a whole culture." — ***Anthony Burgess***[11]

---

[11] Bodin, Y., & Bodin, Y. (2020, December 12). *Quote about Translation - Anthony Burgess | Yolaine Bodin.* Yolaine Bodin. https://yolainebodin.com/the-langu age-nook/quotes/quote-by-anthony-burgess-about-translation

8

Astral Amalgamation - Illuminating Paths of Plurality

In humanity's constant evolution, cultural fusion stands as a display to the growing expansion of cultures, from one end of our globe to the other. This phenomenon, where cultural threads intertwine to create something uniquely new, speaks to the power of hybridity. It is within this blend of identities and perspectives that the beauty of cultural fusion emerges, crafting novel expressions and redefining what it means to belong.

Cultural hybridity, at its core, is the process through which individuals and communities meld aspects of different cultures, forging new identities that transcend traditional boundaries. This synthesis is not merely an amalgamation of disparate elements but a dynamic, evolving creation that embodies the essence of the cultures it draws from. In a world increasingly interconnected through globalization, cultural fusion becomes a vital narrative, reflecting the fluidity of identity and the ever-changing nature of cultural landscapes.

In the realm of human creativity, diversity serves as a wellspring of inspiration, fueling innovation and fostering artistic expression. The process of creating synthesis from diversity is not merely an act of blending various elements but a celebration of the infinite possibilities that arise when different cultural influences intersect. This dynamic interplay between cultures enhances the richness of our creative endeavors, driving us to explore new horizons and reimagine traditional boundaries.

The wealth of human creativity thrives on the diverse cultural influences that inform it. Each culture brings its unique perspectives, traditions, and aesthetic sensibilities, contributing to a global mosaic of artistic expression. This diversity is evident in every form of creativity, from cuisine to visual arts, music to literature, and beyond. When artists, musicians, writers, and creators draw from a multitude of cultural sources, they infuse their work with a depth and complexity that transcends the limitations of a single cultural viewpoint.

Consider the phenomenon of culinary fusion, where the blending of diverse gastronomic traditions results in innovative and exciting flavors. The rise of fusion cuisine, such as Korean tacos or sushi burritos, exemplifies how culinary practices from different corners of the world can come together, creating dishes that honor their origins while presenting something entirely new. These culinary creations not only tantalize the taste buds but also serve as a metaphor for the broader cultural exchanges taking place in our global society. They are a celebration of diversity, illustrating how cultural fusion can lead to richer, more vibrant experiences.

Similarly, the world of music offers a compelling example of cultural fusion. Genres like jazz, reggae, and hip-hop have roots in the blending of African, Caribbean, and American musical traditions. Jazz, with its improvisational nature, emerged from the African American experience, incorporating elements of African rhythms, European harmonic structures, and American folk music. This fusion created a genre that is both deeply rooted in tradition and continually evolving, a symbol of the creative potential inherent in cultural hybridity. Reggae, born from the fusion of Caribbean rhythms and American jazz and blues, gave voice to the struggles and aspirations of the Jamaican people, resonating globally with its messages of resistance and hope. Hip-hop, originating in the Bronx, synthesized the African American musical heritage with the spoken word traditions of the African diaspora, creating a powerful cultural movement that has influenced countless other genres and continues to evolve.

Continuing in the realm of music, the fusion of diverse cultural influences has given rise to some of the most innovative and influential genres. Afrobeat, pioneered by Nigerian musician Fela Kuti[12], blends traditional African rhythms with jazz, funk, and highlife, creating a sound that is both deeply rooted in African culture and globally appealing. Kuti's music, with its complex polyrhythms and socially conscious lyrics, has inspired countless artists around the world, illustrating how cultural synthesis can lead to powerful new forms of expression. Similarly, the emergence of genres like Latin jazz, which combines

---

[12] Wikipedia contributors. (2024f, May 28). *Fela kuti*. Wikipedia. https://en.w ikipedia.org/wiki/Fela_Kuti

Afro-Cuban rhythms with jazz improvisation, showcases the creative potential that arises when cultures collide and coalesce.

The arts provide another fertile ground for the exploration of cultural fusion. Visual arts, literature, and performance art often reflect the melding of different cultural influences, producing works that challenge traditional notions of identity and belonging. The vibrant murals of Mexican American artists, for instance, often depict a blend of indigenous Mexican symbols, Spanish colonial motifs, and contemporary American themes. These visual narratives offer a rich colorful display of cultural fusion, speaking to the complexities of bicultural identity and the ongoing dialogue between past and present.

Visual arts provide a striking example of how cultural diversity enriches creativity. Artists like Frida Kahlo[13], whose work melds Mexican folk art with surrealism, and Yayoi Kusama[14], who combines traditional Japanese motifs with avant-garde abstraction, demonstrate the profound impact of cultural synthesis. Kahlo's paintings, with their vibrant colors and symbolic imagery, reflect her deep connection to Mexican culture while also addressing universal themes of identity, pain, and resilience. Kusama's installations, characterized by their immersive environments and polka-dot motifs, draw from her Japanese heritage and her personal experiences, creating a unique artistic language that resonates globally.

---

[13] Wikipedia contributors. (2024e, May 27). *Frida Kahlo*. Wikipedia. https://en.wikipedia.org/wiki/Frida_Kahlo

[14] Wikipedia contributors. (2024c, May 20). *Yayoi Kusama*. Wikipedia. https://en.wikipedia.org/wiki/Yayoi_Kusama

In literature, the works of authors like Salman Rushdie and Chimamanda Ngozi Adichie explore the intersections of culture, identity, and migration. Rushdie's "Midnight's Children"[15] weaves together the histories of India and Britain, crafting a narrative that blurs the lines between the two cultures and reflects the hybridity of postcolonial identities. Adichie's novels, such as "Americanah"[16], delve into the experiences of Nigerians in America, highlighting the fluidity of cultural identity and the challenges of navigating multiple cultural landscapes.

Authors who draw from multiple cultural traditions often create works that resonate with a wide range of readers, offering fresh perspectives and insights. The novels of Haruki Murakami[17], for example, blend elements of Japanese culture with Western literary traditions, resulting in a unique narrative style that is both accessible and deeply profound. Murakami's stories, with their surreal landscapes and existential themes, explore the human condition in ways that transcend cultural boundaries, appealing to readers from diverse backgrounds.

Cultural fusion also manifests in everyday practices and social norms. The way we celebrate holidays, dress, and even communicate often reflects a blend of cultural influences. For instance, the celebration of Diwali in countries like the United States and Canada incorporates local customs and traditions,

---

[15] Rushdie, S. (2010). *Midnight's Children: The iconic Booker-prize winning novel, from bestselling author Salman Rushdie.* Random House.

[16] Adichie, C. N. (2013). *Americanah.* HarperCollins UK.

[17] Wikipedia contributors. (2024c, May 20). *Haruki Murakami.* Wikipedia. https://en.wikipedia.org/wiki/Haruki_Murakami

creating a unique fusion that honors the essence of the festival while adapting it to new cultural contexts. Similarly, fashion trends increasingly draw from a global palette, with designers blending elements from various cultures to create innovative and inclusive styles.

Language itself is a powerful indicator of cultural fusion. Pidgins[18] and creoles[19], which develop in multilingual communities, exemplify the blending of linguistic elements from different languages. These new languages often arise from the necessity of communication between diverse groups, evolving over time to become fully developed languages with their own rules and nuances. The emergence of Spanglish, a hybrid of Spanish and English, reflects the lived experiences of bilingual communities in the United States, illustrating how language evolves to meet the needs of its speakers and embody their cultural realities.

One striking example of the resilience of hybrid cultural identities is the Creole culture of Louisiana. Emerging from the intermingling of African, French, Spanish, and Native American influences, Creole culture is a vibrant testament to the power of cultural synthesis. Despite facing significant historical challenges, including colonization, slavery, and segregation, Creole communities have maintained a strong sense of identity and cultural cohesion. This hardiness is evident

---

[18] Wikipedia contributors. (2024b, May 21). *Pidgin*. Wikipedia. https://en.wikipedia.org/wiki/Pidgin

[19] Wikipedia contributors. (2024a, January 1). *Creole*. Wikipedia. https://en.wikipedia.org/wiki/Creole

in their rich traditions of music, cuisine, language, and social customs. The Creole language itself, a blend of French and African linguistic elements, symbolizes the adaptive nature of this culture, enabling communication and cohesion among diverse groups.

The Jewish diaspora offers another compelling case study in the suppleness and stability of hybrid cultural identities. Throughout history, Jewish communities have been dispersed across the globe, often facing persecution and displacement. Despite these challenges, they have maintained a strong sense of cultural identity by synthesizing elements from their host cultures with their own traditions. This ability to integrate has enabled Jewish communities to thrive in diverse environments, from Europe to the Middle East to the Americas.

One notable example is the Sephardic Jewish[20] community, which developed a unique cultural identity through its interactions with Muslim and Christian societies in medieval Spain. This synthesis is evident in Sephardic music, which incorporates elements of Spanish, Arabic, and Hebrew traditions, creating a rich and evocative sound. Similarly, Sephardic cuisine blends Spanish and Middle Eastern flavors, resulting in dishes that reflect the community's diverse heritage. The adaptability of Sephardic Jews is further illustrated by their successful integration into new societies following their expulsion from Spain in 1492, as they established thriving communities in places like North Africa, the Ottoman Empire, and later, the

---

[20] Wikipedia contributors. (2024l, May 31). *Sephardic Jews - Wikipedia*. https://en.wikipedia.org/wiki/Sephardic_Jews

Americas.

The digital age has accelerated the process of cultural fusion, enabling instantaneous exchanges of ideas and traditions across the globe. Social media platforms, online forums, and digital content allow individuals to share their cultural expressions and engage with others from diverse backgrounds. This digital interconnectedness fosters a global community where cultural fusion is not only possible but inevitable, as people continuously draw inspiration from and contribute to a shared cultural milieu.

In the realm of education, cultural fusion offers opportunities for enriching the learning experience. Multicultural education, which incorporates elements from various cultural traditions, helps students develop a broader perspective and fosters an appreciation for diversity. By exposing students to different cultural narratives, educators can cultivate an environment of inclusivity and empathy, preparing them to navigate and contribute to a multicultural world.

Cultural fusion also has significant implications for identity formation. For individuals living at the intersection of multiple cultures, navigating their hybrid identities can be both challenging and empowering. The ability to draw from diverse cultural reservoirs enables individuals to develop a multifaceted sense of self, capable of adapting to various social contexts. This fluidity of identity, characteristic of cultural chameleons, becomes a source of strength and resilience, allowing individuals to bridge cultural divides and foster cross-cultural understanding.

Moreover, cultural fusion can drive social innovation and economic development. Cities that embrace cultural diversity often become hubs of creativity and entrepreneurship, attracting talent from around the world. The cross-pollination of ideas and perspectives in such environments leads to the emergence of innovative solutions to complex social and economic challenges. This dynamic interplay of cultures can spark new industries, create jobs, and enhance the quality of life for all residents.

In the corporate world, cultural fusion can enhance organizational effectiveness and competitiveness. Companies that foster inclusive workplaces, where diverse cultural perspectives are valued and integrated, often experience higher levels of creativity, employee engagement, and customer satisfaction. By embracing cultural diversity, businesses can better understand and serve a global customer base, positioning themselves for success in an increasingly interconnected marketplace.

However, the blending of cultures is not without its challenges. The process of cultural fusion can sometimes lead to tensions and conflicts, as individuals and communities navigate the complexities of maintaining their cultural heritage while embracing new influences. Issues of cultural appropriation and the commodification of cultural practices often arise, highlighting the need for sensitivity and respect in the process of cultural exchange. It is crucial to approach cultural fusion with a mindset of mutual respect and understanding, recognizing the value and significance of each culture involved.

The journey of cultural fusion is an ongoing process, continually shaped by the ebb and flow of human interactions. As people move across borders, both physical and metaphorical, they carry with them their cultural heritage, contributing to the ever-evolving mosaic of human society. This continuous blending of identities and perspectives enriches our collective experience, offering new possibilities for connection, creativity, and growth.

The process of creating synthesis from diversity involves more than just combining different cultural elements; it requires a deep understanding and appreciation of the cultures involved. To effectively embrace and celebrate cultural diversity in creative endeavors, artists and creators must adopt strategies that promote inclusivity, respect, and collaboration. One such strategy is cultural immersion, where creators actively engage with and learn from the cultures they seek to incorporate into their work. This can involve traveling to different regions, studying traditional art forms, participating in cultural rituals, and building relationships with local artists and communities.

Hybrid cultures stand as a testament to agility and toughness inherent in human societies. They are vibrant, dynamic entities born from the confluence of different cultural streams, constantly evolving and thriving through the creative synthesis of diverse traditions and perspectives. The power of hybrid cultures lies in their ability to evolve innovate, and flourish in the face of changing environments and shifting social landscapes. This section delves into the resilience and adaptability of hybrid cultural identities, examining case studies of communities that have successfully navigated the complexities of cultural synthesis and emerged stronger and more cohesive.

In contemporary times, hybrid cultures continue to demonstrate remarkable plasticity and persistence in the face of globalization and migration. The multicultural landscape of modern cities like London, New York, and Toronto showcases the power of cultural synthesis in fostering vibrant and dynamic communities. These cities are home to diverse populations that blend their cultural traditions to create new forms of expression and social cohesion.

Toronto, for example, is renowned for its multiculturalism, with over half of its population born outside of Canada. This diversity is reflected in the city's cultural scene, where festivals, food, art, and music from around the world coexist and intermingle. The annual Toronto International Film Festival (TIFF) is a microcosm of this cultural fusion, showcasing films from diverse backgrounds and fostering cross-cultural dialogue. The city's neighborhoods, each with its distinct cultural character, illustrate how hybrid identities contribute to social resilience and economic vitality.

My own experience with cultural fusion was one I sought out, yet I may not have fully comprehended its depth until I was deeply immersed in the vibrant, dynamic city of Hong Kong, where East meets West. This bustling metropolis offered a unique window into the power and complexity of cultural synthesis. From the moment I arrived, I was swept into a world where tradition and modernity coexisted in fascinating harmony.

One of the most striking contrasts was in the realm of business and daily life. It was common to see businessmen dressed in impeccably tailored suits made from fabrics woven in the UK and Italy, sitting side by side at lunchtime. Some chose the simplicity of plastic chairs, enjoying their meal with chopsticks at a local dai pai dong, while others opted for the opulence of a Michelin-starred restaurant, complete with formal table settings. This juxtaposition of casual and sophisticated dining encapsulated the cultural fusion that permeated every aspect of life in Hong Kong.

The architectural landscape of the city further highlighted this blend. Towering metal and glass skyscrapers dominated the skyline, their sleek, modern designs overlooking bustling night markets below. These markets were a sensory explosion, offering an array of funky street foods that reflected Hong Kong's diverse culinary heritage. From the intense negotiations on the trading floors to the lively haggling over a silk robe in the market stalls, the city's economic activities were a testament to its hybrid cultural identity. The transition from the grandeur of marble-clad hotels, where high tea was an elegant affair, to the vibrant street vendors selling that night's stir fry, showcased the integration of different worlds.

Language played a crucial role in my experience of cultural fusion in Hong Kong. The air was constantly filled with a mixture of English expressions and Cantonese words, and I found myself attempting to grasp this linguistic blend, sometimes successfully. The unique approach to queuing, where some adhered strictly to lines and others did not, added to the city's distinctive character. Even the naming of Asian attractions with English names reflected the cultural amalgamation that defined the city.

In Hong Kong, the fusion of cultures was not merely a backdrop but a living, breathing entity that shaped every interaction and experience. This dynamic interplay of traditions and modernity, of East and West, created a vibrant exhibit of life that was both complex and exhilarating. Through my time in Hong Kong, I came to appreciate the dexterity and determination of hybrid cultures, understanding that they are not just a blend of influences but a powerful force that fosters innovation, creativity, and social cohesion.

In conclusion, cultural fusion is a powerful force that shapes our world in profound ways. It reflects the human spirit, as individuals and communities navigate the complexities of blending diverse cultural influences. Through the examples of culinary innovation, musical genres, visual arts, literature, and everyday practices, we see the transformative potential of cultural hybridity. While the process of cultural fusion presents challenges, it also offers opportunities for enrichment, understanding, and innovation. By embracing the dynamic interplay of cultures, we can create a more inclusive and vibrant world, where the beauty of our diverse identities and perspectives shines brightly.

"We have become not a melting pot but a beautiful mosaic. Different people, different beliefs, different yearnings, different hopes, different dreams." – Jimmy Carter[21]

---

[21] *Jimmy Carter | Friends of Silence.* (n.d.). https://friendsofsilence.net/quote/a uthor/jimmy-carter

9

Global Citizenship - A Lifelong Commitment

As Cultural Chameleons, we embark on journeys not merely to collect passport stamps or capture picturesque moments but to undergo profound personal transformations. Each interaction, each new experience, leaves an indelible mark on our souls, shaping us into more enriched and empathetic beings. Yet, the true essence of our travels lies not solely in the distant landscapes we explore, but in how we integrate the lessons learned into the fabric of our everyday lives.

Reflecting on personal growth is akin to gazing into a mirror that reflects not just our physical appearance but the depth of our inner selves. It's about delving beneath the surface and embracing the changes that cultural engagements evoke within us. Whether it's the newfound courage to navigate unfamiliar streets in a foreign land or the humility gained from immersing ourselves in diverse customs and traditions, every encounter leaves an imprint on our journey of self-discovery. Encouraging readers to engage in introspection, we invite them to reflect on the pivotal moments and profound insights gleaned from their travels and experiences . Through this reflective process, they can unearth the gems of wisdom buried within, and discern the currents that direct their personal narratives.

Moreover, reflection isn't a static exercise; it's a dynamic process of self-discovery and growth. It's about examining not just the surface-level observations but delving deeper into the underlying emotions, beliefs, and values that shape our perceptions of the world. By peeling back the layers of our trials, we can gain a deeper understanding of ourselves and our place in the world. From the exhilarating highs of summiting a mountain peak to the humbling lows of navigating a foreign language barrier, each moment offers a window into our innermost thoughts and desires.

Yet, reflection alone is not enough. To truly embody the ethos of Cultural Chameleons, one must transcend the confines of introspection and actively integrate these lessons into the workings of everyday life. Techniques for integrating these insights abound, from the simple act of incorporating foreign cuisine into one's culinary repertoire to the more profound practice of embracing alternative perspectives in decision-making processes. By infusing our daily routines with the essence of our journeys, of both mental and physical realms, we not only honor the moments that have shaped us but also imbue our lives with a sense of purpose and meaning.

Just as cultural fusion catalyzes innovation and economic development on a societal level, so too can it enhance our personal and professional lives. In the corporate realm, embracing diversity isn't merely a matter of ticking boxes on a diversity and inclusion checklist; it's about harnessing the power of cultural synergy to drive organizational effectiveness and competitiveness. Companies that foster inclusive workplaces, where diverse cultural perspectives are valued and integrated, often experience higher levels of creativity, employee engagement, and customer satisfaction. By embracing cultural diversity, businesses can better understand and serve a global customer base, positioning themselves for success in an increasingly interconnected marketplace.

Moreover, the benefits of cultural integration extend far beyond the corporate boardroom. They permeate every aspect of our lives, from the relationships we cultivate to the communities we inhabit. By embracing diversity in all its forms, we not only enrich our own lives but also contribute to the collective tapestry of humanity. Whether it's through volunteering with local immigrant communities or participating in cultural exchange programs, there are countless ways to foster understanding and appreciation in our daily lives. In doing so, we create a more inclusive and harmonious world for future generations to inherit.

In essence, *"Global Citizenship - A Lifelong Commitment"* is not just a chapter title; it's a call to action. It's a reminder that our journeys don't end when we return home; they merely take on a new form. By reflecting on our encounters, integrating the lessons learned, and embracing cultural diversity in all its forms, we can continue to grow and evolve as individuals and as global citizens. So let us embark on this journey together, creating avenues of our diverse experiences into which others may come to further appreciate the human story.

Imagine stepping off a bustling street in Bangkok, where the air is thick with the aroma of exotic spices, only to find yourself navigating the labyrinthine corridors of a crowded subway station in Tokyo the next day. Such is the life of a Cultural Chameleon, constantly adapting to new environments and embracing the diversity of the world around them. Yet, the true test of our cultural acumen lies not in the grand adventures abroad but in the everyday interactions and challenges we encounter when returning to our own communities. In this second part of our journey, we delve into practical tips and strategies for applying the adaptability skills acquired through travel to our daily lives, fostering a global mindset, and embracing diversity in all aspects of life.

We possess a unique set of skills honed through our ventures navigating foreign lands and bridging divides. These skills, from effective communication to flexibility in problem-solving, are not just confined to the realm of other geographies ; they are invaluable assets that can be applied to everyday challenges and interactions. Take, for instance, the art of nonverbal communication, which we often rely on when language barriers stand in our way during our travels. The subtle nuances of body language and facial expressions can speak volumes, transcending linguistic boundaries and fostering connection with those from different cultural backgrounds. By honing our awareness of nonverbal cues in our daily interactions, we can enhance our ability to connect with others and navigate social situations with ease.

Adaptability is a hallmark of the Cultural Chameleon, allowing us to thrive in ever-changing environments. Whether it's navigating a crowded market in Marrakech or navigating the complexities of a high-impact workplace, the ability to adapt and improvise is key to our success. One practical tip for cultivating adaptability in everyday life is to embrace a mindset of curiosity and openness to new experiences. Rather than viewing change as a source of stress or uncertainty, we can approach it as an opportunity for growth and exploration. By reframing our perspective and embracing the unknown, we can turn everyday challenges into opportunities for personal and professional development.

Furthermore, fostering a global mindset is essential for navigating an increasingly interconnected world and embracing diversity in all its forms. This mindset goes beyond mere tolerance or acceptance; it entails actively seeking out opportunities to engage with diverse perspectives and cultures, both at home and abroad. One strategy for fostering such a thought process is to cultivate a curiosity about the world around us, seeking out opportunities for knowledge exchange and learning. Whether it's attending cultural festivals, participating in language exchange programs, or simply striking up conversations with strangers from different backgrounds, there are countless ways to expand our horizons and embrace the richness of human diversity

Embracing diversity is not just a matter of passive acceptance; it requires active engagement and advocacy for social justice and equality. We can use our influence to amplify the voices of those who are marginalized and advocate for a more inclusive and equitable society. This may involve speaking out against discrimination and injustice, supporting initiatives that promote diversity and inclusion, and actively seeking out opportunities to create positive change in our communities. By standing in solidarity with those who are marginalized, we can create a more just and compassionate world for all.

The essence of a global mindset lies not just in the physical act of traversing continents and crossing borders but in the way we view the world around us. It's about recognizing our interconnectedness with people from diverse backgrounds and embracing the beauty of human diversity. Travel experiences serve as catalysts for this mindset, offering glimpses into the lives and cultures of those who inhabit distant lands. Yet, sustaining a global perspective requires more than just passport stamps and souvenir trinkets; it requires a commitment to lifelong learning and an openness to new experiences.

One key aspect of maintaining a global mindset is cultivating an awareness of global issues and trends that transcend geographical boundaries. From climate change and environmental degradation to economic inequality and social injustice, the challenges facing our world are inherently interconnected. By staying informed about these issues and engaging in meaningful dialogue with others, we can broaden our understanding of the complex web of interdependencies that shape our global community. This may involve reading diverse perspectives, attending lectures and workshops, or participating in online forums and discussions. By staying engaged with the world around us, we can cultivate a deeper sense of empathy and compassion for those whose experiences may differ from our own.

In an increasingly interconnected world, technology has become a powerful tool for staying connected to diverse cultures and communities. Social media platforms, online forums, and virtual reality experiences offer unprecedented opportunities for cross-cultural exchange and collaboration. Whether it's connecting with friends and acquaintances from around the world or participating in virtual cultural events and workshops, technology has the potential to bridge geographical divides and foster meaningful connections across cultures. Yet, it's important to approach technology with intentionality and mindfulness, using it as a means to deepen our understanding of the world rather than as a substitute for genuine human connection.

Furthermore, sustaining a global mindset requires a commitment to lifelong learning and personal growth. This may involve seeking out opportunities for formal education and training in global issues and intercultural communication or simply cultivating a spirit of curiosity and openness to new experiences. By embracing a growth mindset and viewing every encounter as an opportunity for learning, we can continue to expand our horizons and deepen our understanding of the world around us. Whether it's through traveling to new destinations, learning a new language, or participating in intercultural exchange programs, there are countless ways to nurture our global mindset and foster connections with diverse cultures and communities.

Personally, those early days of navigating European airports as an unaccompanied minor, produced a journey of human observation and cultural immersion that would shape my understanding of the world. Witnessing the varied reactions of travelers, from the jittery to the serene, I became attuned to the subtleties of human behavior. This experience was my first lesson in the importance of empathy and adaptability.

By the age of 12, my familiarity with airports across Europe was almost second nature. Directing hurried travelers to their gates with an ease that often surprised them, I reveled in the appreciation they showed for my help. These moments of connection, brief as they were, taught me the value of assisting others in their moments of need.

One of the most profound lessons came from immersing myself in the company of those who had little by Western standards. These encounters, often in places far removed from the comforts of home, provided insights into life and gratitude that surpassed anything I had learned in my professional years. The simplicity and resilience of these individuals showed me a different perspective on contentment and fulfillment.

Pushing through mental and physical challenges, particularly those experienced at high altitudes, revealed a resolve within me that I had not known existed. These hardships were not just tests of endurance but also of character, shaping my ability to cope with and overcome adversity.

Through these experiences, I began to understand the importance of living in the present while managing the aspects of life that could shape a better future. Reflecting on my interactions and the lessons learned from diverse cultures, I recognized how these experiences could enhance my perspective and improve my ability to be a better person.

Global citizenship is not a destination but a lifelong journey. It is a continuous process of learning, adapting, and growing. Each experience, each interaction, and each hardship contributes to a deeper understanding of ourselves and the world around us. Embracing this journey with an open mind and a compassionate heart allows us to become true Cultural Chameleons, capable of thriving in any environment while contributing positively to the global community.

"Wherever you go becomes a part of you somehow." - Anita Desai[22]

---

[22] Icharlestondublin. (2016, November 15). *"Wherever you go becomes a part of you somehow."-Anita Desai.* iCharleston DBS. https://icharlestondublin.wor dpress.com/2016/11/15/wherever-you-go-becomes-a-part-of-you-someh ow-anita-desai/

10

Conclusion

As I pen down this final chapter, I am reminded of Ibn Battuta[23]'s profound words: "Traveling – it leaves you speechless, then turns you into a storyteller."[24] This sentiment encapsulates the essence of "Cultural Chameleons: The Traveler's Adaptability Path to Embracing Diversity." The journey through these pages has mirrored the transformative power of exploration, introspection, and revelation.

We began by acknowledging the reality our globalized world, where our destinies are interwoven more closely than ever before. In this interconnected reality, adaptability emerges as an essential skill, not just for personal enrichment but for professional success as well. Those who embrace it, set a

---

[23] Wikipedia contributors. (2024k, May 31). *Ibn Battuta - Wikipedia*. https://en.wikipedia.org/wiki/Ibn_Battuta

[24] Davis, V. a. P. B. M. (2019, July 20). *Traveling: It leaves you speechless, then turns you into a storyteller*. M.L. Davis Writer. https://uninspiredwriters.wordpress.com/2019/07/21/travelling-it-leaves-you-speechless-then-turns-you-into-a-storyteller/

powerful example for us all. This book aims to inspire readers to seize the opportunities that travel and cultural encounters present, developing such skills that enhance their lives and motivate others to embrace the world with open minds and hearts.

In exploring the core of adaptability, we uncovered the resilience, openness, and flexibility required to navigate diverse environments. Travel, as a catalyst for dexterity, exposes us to new experiences and challenges, fostering a spirit of resilience and flexibility essential in our rapidly changing world. The ever-evolving landscapes and the multifaceted tapestry of humanity we encounter demand that we grow, evolve, and transform. This growth is not a passive process but an active engagement with the world around us, requiring conscious effort and a deep-seated willingness to evolve.

We then delved into the beauty of cultural diversity, highlighting the significance of cultural awareness and empathy in bridging divides and fostering understanding. Overcoming stereotypes and biases through genuine interactions allows us to build cultural competence and sensitivity, enriching our lives and the lives of those we encounter. Cultural awareness is not a superficial understanding but a profound appreciation of the richness and complexity of different ways of life. It involves recognizing the intrinsic value of diverse cultural expressions and understanding how they contribute to the collective human experience.

We addressed the inevitable challenges of cultural immersion, emphasizing the importance of preparing for these experiences, coping with culture shock, and developing strategies for adaptation. Commitment and a willingness to learn from cultural differences are crucial in embracing new environments. Culture shock is not merely a momentary discomfort but a profound realignment of our perceptions and expectations. It challenges our preconceived notions and forces us to confront the limits of our understanding. In this confrontation lies the potential for profound personal growth and transformation.

Profound lessons are learned from engaging with local communities, providing invaluable insights into different ways of life and enhancing our cross-cultural communication skills. Finding common ground amidst diversity helps us connect on a human level, reinforcing the universal aspects of our shared humanity. Engaging with local communities involves more than just surface-level interactions; it requires a deep immersion into the everyday lives of people, understanding their struggles, aspirations, and joys. It is through these meaningful connections that we gain a deeper appreciation of the common threads that bind us all.

We explored the innovative potential of diversity, showcasing how adapting to unfamiliar environments and collaborating across cultures fosters creativity and problem-solving skills. By leveraging diversity, we unlock new avenues for innovation and success, as evidenced by numerous case studies of multicultural collaborations. Diversity is not just a source of richness but a catalyst for innovation. When we bring together different perspectives and ways of thinking, we create fertile ground for creativity and new ideas to flourish. This synergy is the driving force behind many of the world's most significant advancements and breakthroughs.

We emphasized the evolution that comes from embracing discomfort and overcoming misunderstandings. Resilience and perseverance are key to navigating cross-cultural interactions and managing conflicts. These experiences teach us the transformative power of stepping outside our comfort zones and embracing the unknown. Embracing discomfort is not about seeking out hardship but about recognizing that true growth often comes from pushing beyond our limits. It involves a willingness to be vulnerable, to make mistakes, and to learn from those experiences. In this process, we develop the resilience and perseverance necessary to navigate the complexities of the world.

We celebrated the richness of cultural hybridity, where the blending of identities and perspectives leads to the emergence of new cultural expressions and creative endeavors. By embracing and celebrating diversity, we contribute to the quick-wittedness and staying power of hybrid cultural identities, showcasing communities that thrive through cultural synthesis. Cultural hybridity is a testament to the dynamic and ever-evolving nature of human societies. It reflects the ongoing interplay between different cultural influences and the ways in which they shape and reshape our identities. This blending creates new forms of cultural expression that are both unique and reflective of the diverse influences that contribute to their creation.

Reflecting on personal growth and integrating the lessons learned into everyday life is a lifelong journey. Fostering a global mindset and embracing diversity in all aspects of life ensures that we maintain a global perspective, enriching our lives and those of future generations. Personal growth is not a finite destination but an ongoing process of learning and self-discovery. It involves continually challenging ourselves to grow, adapt, and evolve in response to the changing world around us. By embracing this journey, we cultivate a deeper understanding of ourselves and our place in the world.

As we conclude this exploration, I extend my heartfelt gratitude to you, the reader, for sharing in these experiences. Your journey through these pages reflects a commitment to understanding and embracing the world's rich tapestry of cultures. Let these stories and insights inspire you to become a Cultural Chameleon, open-hearted and ready to navigate and celebrate the diverse world around you. Being a cultural chameleon is not about losing oneself but about enriching one's identity through the incorporation of diverse influences. It involves a willingness to embrace change, to learn from different perspectives, and to grow in response to new experiences.

Ibn Battuta's words remind us that travel transforms us, turning us into storytellers. As you continue your journey, may you carry these stories with you, sharing them with others and inspiring a more understanding and connected world. These life events are not just about visiting new places but about the transformation that occurs within us as a result of those experiences. It is about the stories we gather, the lessons we learn, and the ways in which those interactions shape our understanding of the world and our place in it. By sharing these stories, we contribute to a collective understanding that transcends cultural and geographical boundaries.

Embracing the world around us does not necessitate trips around the globe; it can start simply by interacting with those within our community. Mainstream media might have us believe that the world is dangerous and that other cultures are in the wrong, creating false narratives for their own benefit. Recent events, such as the pandemic and the attempted division of society through forced confinement and control, should make us aware that we are stronger united than apart.

My words in these passages were intended to motivate others to seek opportunities that alter their current state, produce teaching moments for the future, and create lasting memories to share as stories with those around them. We have all come through some difficult years recently; our current state is volatile, with many cultures clashing and significant shifts of power palpable. Humanity has always gone through cycles of peaks and troughs, and we are no different and current difficulties shall pass.

As we continue to evolve, one aspect of conversations that I find particularly concerning is our capacity for open discussion. Simply because I don't agree with someone does not mean I don't like them. Time is a commodity we are not making more of; use it wisely, cherish it, and embrace your mortality. The past can be learned from but not dwelled on, and worrying about matters you cannot control is a waste of energy you could direct towards something meaningful.

Thank you for embarking on this journey with me. Safe travels, and may your adaptability guide you to endless horizons of discovery and growth.

Also by Cliffton Santiago

**Summits of Resilience
A Journey Through Life's Challenges**

In "Summits of Resilience," readers embark on an exploration of the human spirit through a captivating collection of personal narratives. Traverse the highs and lows of life's journey, finding inspiration in tales of triumph over adversity.

Each story serves as a beacon of hope, offering profound lessons on perseverance in the face of life's greatest challenges. As you immerse yourself in these pages, discover the transformative power of endurance and the boundless potential within each of us to rise above even the most daunting obstacles.

Find inspiration in stories of triumph over adversity.

Explore the transformative power of resilience in the human experience.

Discover profound lessons on perseverance and endurance.

www.ingramcontent.com/pod-product-compliance
Lightning Source LLC
Chambersburg PA
CBHW052109150726
48002CB00006B/2275